# BATMAN:
## THE COURT OF OWLS SAGA

SCOTT SNYDER writer GREG CAPULLO penciller
JONATHAN GLAPION inker

"The Call" & "The Fall of the House of Wayne"

JAMES TYNION IV co-writer RAFAEL ALBUQUERQUE artist

FCO PLASCENCIA NATHAN FAIRBAIRN DAVE McCAIG colorists

RICHARD STARKINGS COMICRAFT'S JIMMY BETANCOURT

PAT BROSSEAU DEZI SIENTY letterers

BATMAN created by BOB KANE with BILL FINGER

THE COURT OF OWLS created by SCOTT SNYDER and GREG CAPULLO

Collection cover art by GREG CAPULLO and FCO PLASCENCIA

**BATMAN: THE COURT OF OWLS SAGA: DC COMPACT COMICS EDITION**

Published by DC Comics. Compilation and all new material Copyright © 2024 DC Comics. All Rights Reserved. Originally published in single magazine form in *Batman* 1-11. Copyright © 2011, 2012 DC Comics. All Rights Reserved. All characters, their distinctive likenesses, and related elements featured in this publication are trademarks of DC Comics. The stories, characters, and incidents featured in this publication are entirely fictional. DC Comics does not read or accept unsolicited submissions of ideas, stories, or artwork. DC Comics, 4000 Warner Blvd., Bldg. 700, 2nd Floor, Burbank, CA 91522. Printed by Solisco Printers, Scott, QC, Canada. 3/5/26. Sixth Printing. ISBN: 978-1-77952-727-1.

Library of Congress Cataloging-in-Publication Data is available.

FSC www.fsc.org MIX Paper | Supporting responsible forestry FSC® C103304

# CHAPTER ONE • KNIFE TRICK

Every Saturday, the Gotham Gazette includes a small life-styles piece called "Gotham Is."
In the column, random Gothamites are asked to complete the sentence "Gotham is..." using three words or less.
The Gazette has been running the "Gotham Is" column for years, ever since I was a **boy.**
MAJE TIC
T EA RE
Here are some of the words used to describe Gotham the past few weeks:
"Damned."
"Cursed."
"Bedlam."
"Murderous..."

Gotham is "villainous."
Gotham is "a losing game."
Gotham is "hopeless."
ProF

YOU'RE ALL OURS, NOW.
NO WAY OUT, BATS.
-SIGH- THERE'S NO PLACE LIKE HOME.

Once in a while, someone names one of the city's **villains** as their answer to the "Gotham Is" question.
Usually it's some kid, a teenager going for shock value.
But now and then someone actually tries to make the argument that the city is best reflected in its villains.
For example. "Gotham is ***Two-Face,*** " meaning Gotham is a city at odds with itself.
Or "Gotham is ***Killer Croc.*** "
Meaning the city is little more than a cannibalistic **monster.**

I've seen a few "Mr. Freezes."
Two "Black Masks."
Lately I've seen a couple new names appear, too.
OIN-
But for me, Gotham's criminals...
...whether old...
...or new...
...will never define this city. Because in the end, they're simple and cowardly, ruled by predictable desires.

Granted, now and then, one of them will do something that catches even me off-guard...
I WAS HERE
twice
...something particularly depraved...
...or twisted...
THERE YOU ARE!
AND HERE I WAS BEGINNING TO THINK YOU WERE GOING TO DIE WITHOUT EVEN SAYING GOODBYE!
YOU READY TO DO THIS?
AW, ALWAYS SO SERIOUS.
FINE, THEN...

...LET'S CUT TO THE PUNCH LINE!
JOKER? WHAT ARE YOU DOING, YOU TURNCOAT PIECE OF--
BEHIND YOU!
GOT HIM.
Of course, one of the most common answers to the "Gotham Is" question is "Batman."
Gotham is "Batman."
Gotham is "Batman's city."
Gotham is "the Bat..."
All answers I'm partial to, myself.

Still, I like to think a vote for Batman is a broader affirmation--a vote for all of Gotham's heroes.
A vote for the G.C.P.D.
Honest, tireless men like Commissioner Jim Gordon.
I STILL DON'T UNDERSTAND. A FULL-SCALE BREAKOUT? WITH NO WARNING?
IT WASN'T A BREAKOUT.
I'VE BEEN INVESTIGATING A WEAK LINK AT ARKHAM ASYLUM. A GUARD NAMED MATTHEWS. I WAS COMING FOR HIM.
HE SPRANG THE DOORS TO STOP ME.
NOT DAN MATTHEWS? HE'S ONE OF THE BEST MEN ON PAYROLL THERE...I'VE KNOWN HIM SINCE HE WAS AN ACADEMY BOY.
HE'S GOT A FATHER WITH HEALTH PROBLEMS. A DIVORCE LOOMING.
HE AND BELLE ARE GETTING DIVORCED?
I HAD NO IDEA.
NEITHER DOES SHE.
GEEZ. WHO'S THE NEW PAL?
COCKTAIL WAITRESS. ICEBERG LOUNGE. IMPRESSIVE SHEET OF HER OWN.

AND YOU FOUND HIM OUT **HOW?** YOU HAD A MAN ON THE INSIDE?
SOMETHING LIKE THAT.
DAN MATTHEWS ON THE TAKE AT ARKHAM...
...THERE'S NOBODY THE SCUM OF GOTHAM CAN'T GET TO, IS THERE?
I WOULDN'T SAY THAT.
ONE MORE THING. ON THE CC FOOTAGE, IT ALMOST LOOKS YOU'RE FIGHTING ***ALONGSIDE*** THE JOKER.
TELL ME THAT'D BE RIDICULOUS.
THAT'D BE RIDICULOUS, JIM.
THAT'S WHAT I FIGURED...
...JUST A SIMPLE TRICK OF THE LIGHT.

SO IT'S TRUE...

...YOU DO ACTUALLY PRACTICE BROODING.
I ALWAYS SUSPECTED.
I'M WORKING.
WITH THE COMPUTER OFF.
SATISFIED?
IMPRESSED.
IT'S A NEW SYSTEM I'M TESTING.
A CONTACT LENS WITH A REMOTE ACCESS PROCESSOR LINKED TO THE COMPUTER DOWN HERE.
AND DICK...
....TAKE OFF THE E.M.P. MASK.

BELIEVE ME, I'VE BEEN *DYING* TO. I JUST WANTED TO MAKE SURE YOU DISCONNECTED IT FROM THE MAIN-FRAME FIRST.
SO...A CONTACT LENS WITH REMOTE ACCESS?
MEANING, ANYWHERE YOU GO, THE *BATCAVE* GOES WITH YOU?
NOW *THAT* SOUNDS HEALTHY.
WE SHOULD GO.
FOR WHAT IT'S WORTH, HOW'D I DO AS HIM?
ARE YOU ASKING ME IF YOU WERE CONVINCING AS A HOMICIDAL MANIAC, DICK?
I SUPPOSE I AM.
THEN YES, AS A MATTER OF FACT, YOU WERE.
SCORE ONE FOR ALFRED'S SCHOOL OF ACTING. STILL, I CAN'T BELIEVE YOU LEFT ME IN THERE AN EXTRA DAY.
I NEEDED TO BE SURE IT WAS MATTHEWS.
BESIDES, WITH ALL YOU'VE BEEN SHOULDERING LATELY, I FIGURED YOU COULD USE THE DAY OFF.
A DAY OFF. IN ARKHAM. ONLY YOU, BRUCE...ONLY YOU.

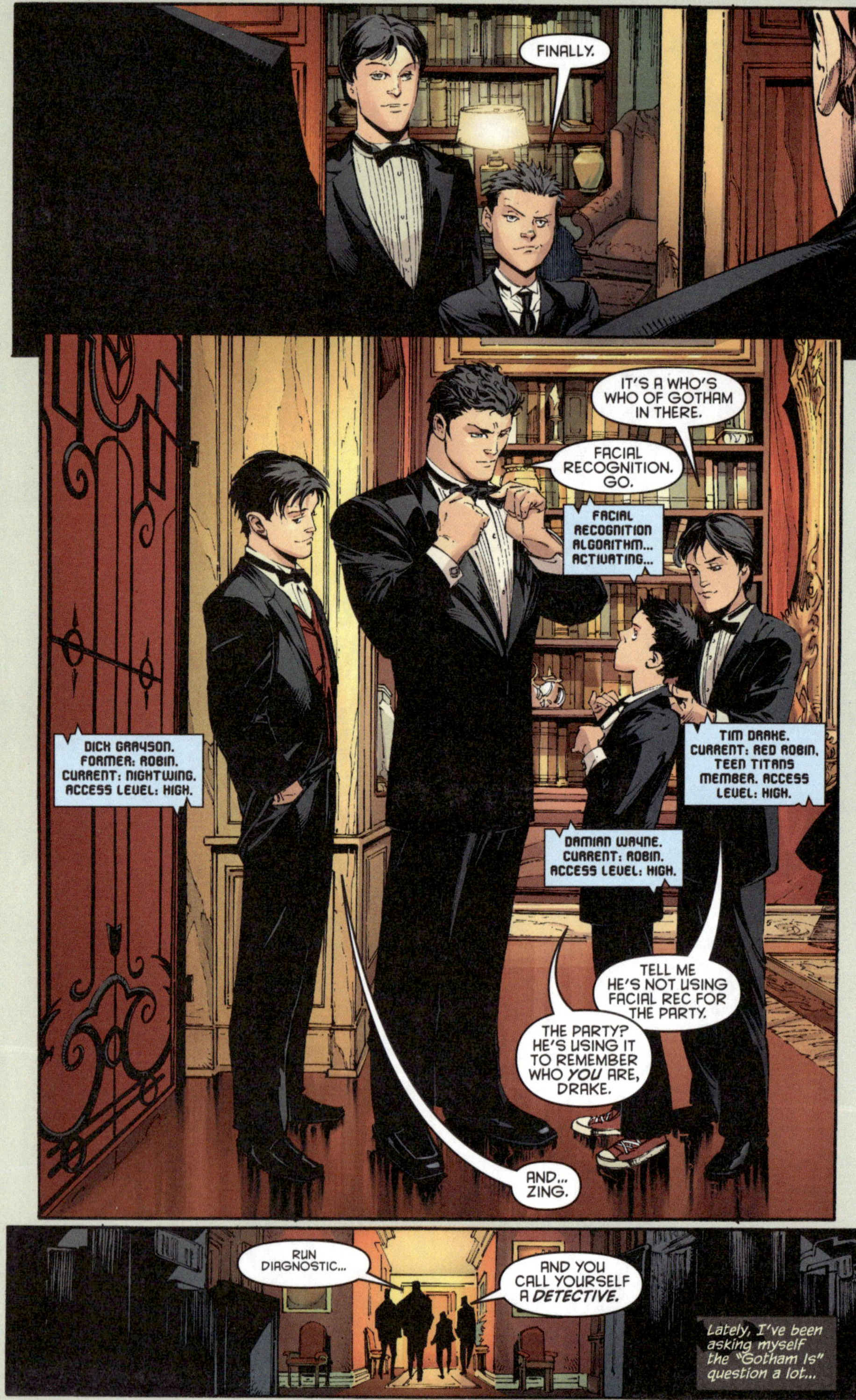
FINALLY.
IT'S A WHO'S WHO OF GOTHAM IN THERE.
FACIAL RECOGNITION. GO.
FACIAL RECOGNITION ALGORITHM... ACTIVATING...
DICK GRAYSON. FORMER: ROBIN. CURRENT: NIGHTWING. ACCESS LEVEL: HIGH.
TIM DRAKE. CURRENT: RED ROBIN, TEEN TITANS MEMBER. ACCESS LEVEL: HIGH.
DAMIAN WAYNE. CURRENT: ROBIN. ACCESS LEVEL: HIGH.
TELL ME HE'S NOT USING FACIAL REC FOR THE PARTY.
THE PARTY? HE'S USING IT TO REMEMBER WHO *YOU* ARE, DRAKE.
AND... ZING.
RUN DIAGNOSTIC...
AND YOU CALL YOURSELF A ***DETECTIVE.***
*Lately, I've been asking myself the "Gotham Is" question a lot...*

...WHAT IS GOTHAM CITY TO ME, BRUCE WAYNE? IN A SINGLE WORD...
HOME? FAMILY?
PURPOSE?
BUT THE TRUTH-- THE REAL TRUTH--IS... I COULDN'T ANSWER THE QUESTION.
BUT THEN I REMEMBERED SOMETHING, FRIENDS. I REMEMBERED SOMETHING MY FATHER, THOMAS WAYNE, USED TO SAY TO ME BEFORE BED SOMETIMES, BACK WHEN I WAS A BOY AND I'D HAD A BAD DAY...
...WHEN I'D FALLEN DOWN A HOLE IN THE GROUND OR SKINNED MY KNEE.
AT THE END OF A DAY LIKE THAT HE'D PAT MY HEAD AND HE'D SAY, "BRUCE, TOMORROW IS ONE DREAM AWAY." THAT WAS HIS PHRASE. SENTIMENTAL, I KNOW. BUT STILL, IT WORKED FOR ME.
NOW, AS MOST OF YOU KNOW, MY FATHER DIED WHEN I WAS JUST A BOY. HE WAS GUNNED DOWN, ALONG WITH MY MOTHER IN CRIME ALLEY ACROSS TOWN.
AND AS YOU CAN IMAGINE, THE DAYS FOLLOWING HIS DEATH WERE THE WORST OF MY LIFE. DAYS OF ANGER AND FEAR AND SADNESS. STILL, THAT PHRASE, MY FATHER'S PHRASE--TOMORROW IS ONE DREAM AWAY-- IT KEPT COMING BACK TO ME...
...AND DEEP DOWN I KNEW, MUCH AS IT HURT RIGHT THEN, THINGS WOULD GET BETTER.
NOW, WHY AM I TELLING YOU THIS? WELL, FRIENDS, MY POINT IS THIS--WHEN CIRCUMSTANCES ARE CHALLENGING, OR FRIGHTENING, ASKING OURSELVES WHAT OUR CITY "IS" IS POINTLESS.
BECAUSE ALL WE WILL SEE, WHEN WE LOOK AROUND AT THE BUILDINGS AND STREETS, WILL BE OUR OWN FEARS, OUR OWN FRUSTRATIONS.
OUR OWN DEMONS.
BUT IF WE STOP LOOKING TO THE PRESENT AND THE PAST, AND INSTEAD WE LOOK TO THE FUTURE...

...IF WE ASK OURSELVES WHAT CAN BE--WHAT WILL BE--TOMORROW... THEN WE'RE ASKING THE RIGHT QUESTION. BECAUSE TO HOPE, TO DREAM, TO PREDICT IS TO SHAPE THE CITY YOURSELF, RATHER THAN TO BE SHAPED BY IT.
SO, PUTTING MY MONEY WHERE MY MOUTH IS...
...NEXT MONTH, WAYNE ENTERPRISES WILL BEGIN INVESTING--AGGRESSIVELY AND IMMEDIATELY--IN GOTHAM'S FUTURE.
WORKING WITH VARIOUS DOMESTIC DESIGN FIRMS, WE'VE ALREADY SET IN MOTION AN INITIATIVE TO REBUILD SOME OF GOTHAM'S MOST DERELICT INDUSTRIAL NEIGHBORHOODS. FROM THERE, WE PLAN ON MOVING BOLDLY TO EXPAND AND MODERNIZE GOTHAM'S PUBLIC TRANSIT SYSTEM.
I CANNOT TELL YOU HOW EXCITED, HOW HOPEFUL I AM ABOUT THESE PLANS. MUCH MORE WILL BE REVEALED IN THE COMING DAYS, BUT FOR NOW, I ASK YOU TO DO THIS...
LOOK PAST WHAT GOTHAM WAS, WHAT GOTHAM IS...AND IMAGINE WITH ME, JUST FOR A MOMENT...
...GOTHAM AS IT WILL BE...
GASP!
THANK YOU... NOW WHAT I ASK OF YOU, FRIENDS, IS TO INVEST WITH ME. INVEST IN GOTHAM'S FUTURE. BECAUSE I PROMISE YOU, IF WE CAN ALL DO THAT, TOGETHER...
CLAP! CLAP!
BRAVO! BRAVO!

"...A BETTER, BRIGHTER GOTHAM IS ONE DREAM AWAY."
ALFRED PENNYWORTH. CARETAKER. WAYNE ESTATE. ACCESS LEVEL: HIGHEST.
WELL DONE, MASTER BRUCE. INSPIRING. THOUGH...
THANK YOU, ALFRED.
THOUGH YOU DID FAIL TO MENTION THE MYRIAD OF NEW BAT-BUNKERS YOU'LL BE BUILDING THROUGHOUT THE CITY.
HUH. MUST HAVE SLIPPED MY MIND. NEXT PRESENTATION MAYBE.
BRUCE! THERE YOU ARE.
VICKI VALE. REPORTER FOR THE GOTHAM GAZETTE.
SO FIRST YOU FUND THE DIGITIZING OF THE GAZETTE, NOW YOU'RE REBUILDING HALF THE CITY...I'D SAY YOU WERE GOTHAM'S OWN MAN OF TOMORROW, THAT IS, IF I WASN'T ALREADY SAYING HE IS.
LINCOLN MARCH, BRUCE WAYNE. LINCOLN IS--
RUNNING FOR MAYOR, YES, I KNOW. AND MARCH VENTURE... YOU UNDERWROTE LESLIE THOMPKINS'S SATELLITE CLINIC ON THE EAST SIDE, DIDN'T YOU?
LINCOLN MARCH. C.O.O. MARCH VENTURE. CURRENT GOTHAM CITY MAYORAL CANDIDATE.
WOW. I'M IMPRESSED.

ANY FRIEND OF LESLIE'S...
DOES THAT MEAN I HAVE YOUR VOTE?
THAT DEPENDS. DO I HAVE YOURS?
ON THIS? I'M CERTAINLY INTERESTED.
CAN I ASK HOW MANY INVESTORS YOU HAVE LINED UP ALREADY?
YOU CAN ASK.
THAT MANY...
LIKE I SAID, WE'VE BEEN AGGRESSIVE IN OUR EFFORTS TO RECRUIT PARTNERS. LUCKILY, THE RESPONSE HAS BEEN LARGELY ENTHUSIASTIC.
WELL, ALL KIDDING ASIDE, I REALLY AM INTERESTED IN PLAYING A PART, BRUCE. CAN WE SET SOMETHING UP?
OF COURSE...WHAT DO YOU HAVE IN MIND?
Breakfast. Or lunch. We could...

-COUGH-COUGH- (LIP READ GO).
I'M SORRY. GO ON.
LIP READ ACTIVATING... OCULAR TARGETING TO...
I WAS JUST SAYING I'M ENTHUSIASTIC TO...
HOW MANY STAB WOUNDS? GOD.
ALL RIGHT, I'LL BE RIGHT DOWN. JUST GIVE ME TEN MINUTES TO ESCAPE FROM PLANET OF THE CREPES.
"CREPE." IT'S A PANCAKE. NEVER MIND.
BRUCE?
I'M SORRY, WHAT?
I WAS SAYING I COULD DO AS EARLY AS TOMORROW. LUNCH? TALK ABOUT YOUR PLANS?
OF COURSE. TOMORROW. ALFRED, SET IT UP, WILL YOU? NOW IF YOU'LL EXCUSE ME FOR A MOMENT, LINCOLN...

"...I NEED TO GET SOME AIR."
NO, YOU RANK STOOGES, PROP THE WEATHER TARP FIRST!
RAINDROPS. EVIDENCE. NO MATCH.
GEEZ, THEY GROW THEM STUPID NOWADAYS.
HELLO, HARVEY.
BACK TO STEALTH MODE, I SEE.
COME ON. LET'S GO LOOK AT SOME ART.

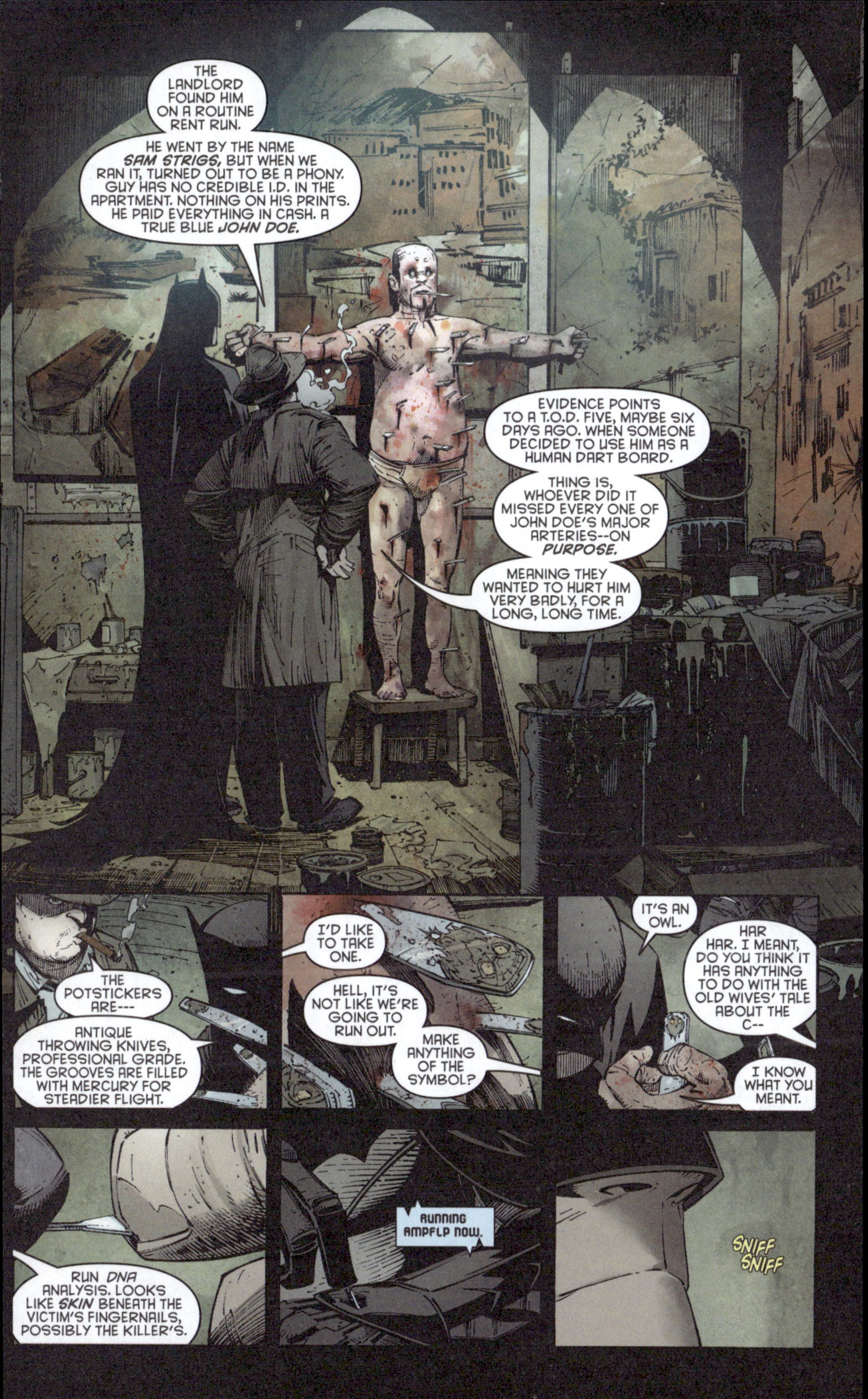
THE LANDLORD FOUND HIM ON A ROUTINE RENT RUN.
HE WENT BY THE NAME SAM STRIGS, BUT WHEN WE RAN IT, TURNED OUT TO BE A PHONY. GUY HAS NO CREDIBLE I.D. IN THE APARTMENT. NOTHING ON HIS PRINTS. HE PAID EVERYTHING IN CASH. A TRUE BLUE JOHN DOE.
EVIDENCE POINTS TO A T.O.D. FIVE, MAYBE SIX DAYS AGO. WHEN SOMEONE DECIDED TO USE HIM AS A HUMAN DART BOARD.
THING IS, WHOEVER DID IT MISSED EVERY ONE OF JOHN DOE'S MAJOR ARTERIES--ON PURPOSE.
MEANING THEY WANTED TO HURT HIM VERY BADLY, FOR A LONG, LONG TIME.
THE POTSTICKERS ARE---
ANTIQUE THROWING KNIVES, PROFESSIONAL GRADE. THE GROOVES ARE FILLED WITH MERCURY FOR STEADIER FLIGHT.
I'D LIKE TO TAKE ONE.
HELL, IT'S NOT LIKE WE'RE GOING TO RUN OUT.
MAKE ANYTHING OF THE SYMBOL?
IT'S AN OWL.
HAR HAR. I MEANT, DO YOU THINK IT HAS ANYTHING TO DO WITH THE OLD WIVES' TALE ABOUT THE C--
I KNOW WHAT YOU MEANT.
RUN DNA ANALYSIS. LOOKS LIKE SKIN BENEATH THE VICTIM'S FINGERNAILS, POSSIBLY THE KILLER'S.
RUNNING AMPFLP NOW.
SNIFF SNIFF

WHAT? WHAT IS IT?
GIVE ME YOUR CIGAR.
MY CIGAR?
THAT SMELL IS LINSEED OIL. A COMMON PAINT THINNER.
BUT THE INTENSITY IS TOO STRONG.
SO OUR GUY SPILLED A CAN OF PAINT THINNER. SO WHAT?
MAYBE...

Bruce Wayne will DIE Tomorrow
...OR MAYBE HE WAS USING IT TO LEAVE A LAST MESSAGE, A WARNING, BEFORE HE WAS MURDERED.
WELL, OUR JOHN DOE WASN'T ANY NOSTRADAMUS, THAT'S FOR SURE.
I'M JUST SAYING, IF OUR TIME OF DEATH FOR HIM WAS A WEEK AGO, THE "TOMORROW" HE THOUGHT WOULD BE WAYNE'S LAST DAY ALREADY CAME AND WENT. SO WAYNE'S IN THE CLEAR.
UNLESS JOHN DOE KNEW WHEN HE'D BE FOUND. YOU SAID THE LANDLORD WAS MAKING A ROUTINE RUN. I ASSUME HE--
ALWAYS CAME ON THE SECOND FRIDAY OF THE MONTH...SO IT'S POSSIBLE OUR VICITIM KNEW HE WAS GOING TO DIE, KNEW HE WAS GOING TO BE FOUND TODAY, AND SO LEFT A WARNING THAT WHOEVER KILLED HIM WOULD BE COMING AFTER WAYNE NEXT.
THEN TO THE KILLER I SAY GOOD LUCK. WAYNE'S SECURITY HAS SECURITY.
ANYONE GOING TO TAKE A CRACK AT THE GUY IS GOING TO HAVE TO BE SOMEONE CLOSE. SOMEONE IN WAYNE'S CIRCLE, WOULD BE MY GUESS.
MAKES YOU ALMOST FEEL BAD FOR THE GUY.
ALMOST?
I KNOW YOU AND WAYNE ARE PALS AND ALL THAT. BUT GUYS LIKE WAYNE, THEY DON'T GET HOW THE CITY WORKS THE WAY WE DO.
I MEAN, I LISTENED TO HIS SPEECH TONIGHT ON THE RADIO. ALL ABOUT WHAT GOTHAM "IS" AND "WAS" AND "WILL BE."

WHEN IT COMES TO GOTHAM, THOUGH--
QUIET.
YOU'RE SURE.
QUITE, SIR. THE SKIN CELLS BENEATH THE VICTIM'S FINGERNAILS CAME BACK A PERFECT MATCH...
LOOK, I DIDN'T MEAN TO KNOCK YOUR BOY WAYNE. I'M JUST SAYING...
"...MY VIEW IS, WHEN IT COMES TO GOTHAM, YOU DON'T KNOW IT, BROTHER. IT KNOWS YOU.
" AND THE MOMENT YOU THINK OTHERWISE, THE MOMENT YOU GET TOO COMFORTABLE...
"...THAT'S WHEN IT STABS YOU RIGHT IN THE BACK."
DNA Match: Dick Grayson
"BECAUSE ABOVE EVERYTHING, GOTHAM IS... A MYSTERY."

# CHAPTER TWO • TRUST FALL

The original Wayne Tower.
If you came to Gotham city today, right now, and took a tour of the building, here are some things your guide would tell you:
The tower was constructed in 1888, under the watch of my great, great grandfather Alan Wayne.
He built the tower to serve as a symbol of welcome to people coming to Gotham. And, as your guide will point out, from the ground up, it's designed to give visitors like you the feeling that they're cared for and protected.
For example, your guide will say, the building has twelve gargoyles or "guardians," as Alan insisted they be called--one to watch over each passageway into the city.
The five guardians at the first tier were placed there to watch over the five original gateways into Gotham--the three bridges and two tunnels.
Higher up the tower is a ring of seven guardians, one to protect each of the seven train lines that converge at Union Station, below Wayne Tower's base.
And at the top of the tower is the observation deck, which Alan insisted remain free and open to the public every weekend, all year round.
For the windows, Alan demanded that only the best glass be used. A kind of double-bonded, laminated float glass, designed to be crystal-quality, weatherproof. And, most important, unbreakable.

Unbreakable, that is, unless--like the assassin who just kicked me through them--you know how to hit the glass just right.
Make impact at the edge of the plate, rather than the center, where it's designed to bend and flex.
The throwing knives are perfectly placed, too. Lodged tight in my brachial arteries.
The pain and blood loss make it almost impossible to grab on to anything to break my fall...
...impossible to do anything.
Except bleed and drop...
...and watch the city rise up to greet me.

24 HOURS EARLIER...
...I'M POSITIVE! I HIT HIM WITH TWO POUNDS OF SEMTEX. TWO POUNDS!
SAY WHAT YOU WANT, I'LL SPIKE THE BALL WHEN WE'RE OVER THE HARBOR. OUR GUY IS SUPPOSED TO BE WAITING JUST PAST THE STRAITS TO TAKE THE STATUES.
WHY ARE WE GOING SO DAMN SLOW? I THOUGHT THIS THING WAS SUPPOSED TO CRUISE AT TWO-HUNDRED KNOTS!
IT IS. BUT HE DESTROYED THE COAXIAL WITH THAT "BAT" THING.
YOU WANT FASTER? DUMP A FEW OF THE PRETTY LADIES.
BUT OUR GUY SAID ALL TEN OF THESE THINGS FROM THE HELLENISTIC WING. TEN.
HE ISN'T THE ONE ABOUT TO GO DOWN IN THE MIDDLE OF THE AVENUE. START TOSSING THEM!
HELL, I NEVER WAS MUCH FOR PALE GIRLS, ANYHOW.
AND AT LEAST THESE ONES WON'T SCREA--
CRASH

AEEEEEEEEEEE!
HE GOT ROLF!
WHAT ARE YOU DOING, MAN? GET THE HELL AWAY FROM HIM! TURN!
SHUT UP! THE BAT WANTS TO PLAY CHICKEN...
...LET'S PLAY CHICKEN.
HOOONNNK
WHAT... WHAT'S HE DOING?

HE WOULDN'T.
VROOMMM
TURN! TURN!
I...I CAN'T, THE DAMN ALLEY'S TOO NARROW!
SIR? COMMISSIONER GORDON HAS ARRIVED AT THE MORGUE.
NOTED, ALFRED.
I'LL BE THERE...
SHALL I ASSUME YOU WON'T BE BACK FOR THE AUTOPSY? I CAN POWER DOWN THE--
BUT, SIR. I HAVE YOU ALL THE WAY OVER ON--
RELAX. THIS'LL ONLY TAKE A MOMENT.

I'M AFRAID THERE'S LITTLE MORE TO RELAY THAN THE OBVIOUS. OUR JOHN DOE WAS STABBED MULTIPLE TIMES, LIKELY IN AN ACT OF TORTURE.
DIED FROM THE ORAL WOUND, HERE, WHICH CAUSED HIM TO HEMORRHAGE INTO HIS OWN THROAT.
CHOKED ON HIS OWN BLOOD...AH, GOTHAM, PLEASANT AS EVER.
I SHOULD BE GOING. THEY'RE WAITING ON ME DOWN IN BURNS. HIT THE LIGHTS ON--
MY WAY OUT. BILL, DON'T YOU THINK I KNOW THE DRILL BY NOW?
'NIGHT, COMMISSIONER.
John Doe
WELL?

...YOU THERE?
I'M HERE, JIM. STEP BACK.
WELL, THAT'S COLORFUL. IT WORK?
READY.
SO WHAT WE HAVE IS A GENUINE *MYSTERY MAN.* PAID HIS RENT IN CASH. NO IDENTIFICATION IN THE PLACE. WE CHECKED HIS DNA AGAINST STATE AND FEDERAL. NOT ONE PING.
WE KNOW *NOTHING* ABOUT HIM. EXCEPT HE MADE A PRETTY DECENT DARTBOARD FOR SOMEONE.
HERE. THERE'S EXTENSIVE SCAR TISSUE AROUND THE RIBS AND ABDOMEN...CALCIFICATION AT HIS BROW, SIDE OF HIS SKULL.
HUH. "THE PUGILIST'S BEAUTY MARKS." YOU THINK OUR JOHN DOE WAS A FIGHTER IN HIS GLORY DAYS?
MAYBE. BUT HE'S GOT MORE CALLOUS MATERIAL AROUND HIS PALMS AND WRISTS THAN HIS KNUCKLES. DEFENSIVE SCARRING.
A *TRAINER...*
THERE ARE *SCARS* ALONG HIS FORE-ARMS. COMMON INJURIES FROM SWORDPLAY.
SO THE GUY IS A HIGH-END TRAINER. HE'S TOUGH, IS THE IDEA.
BUT NOW SOMEONE EVEN TOUGHER, SOMEONE HE KNOWS HE CAN'T BEAT IS COMING FOR HIM.
AND THE MESSAGE HE LEAVES FOR US TO FIND IS *"BRUCE WAYNE WILL DIE TOMORROW."*
IT'S CURIOUS.
I CONTACTED WAYNE, YOU KNOW. ASKED HIM IF HE WANTED POLICE DETAIL FOR THE NEXT TWENTY-FOUR HOURS, BUT HE TURNED ME DOWN.
I TAKE IT YOU'RE KEEPING AN EYE ON HIM?
I HAVE IT COVERED.
JIM, HIS THIRD MOLAR. RIGHT SIDE. THE SCANNER'S PICKING UP AN ABNORMAL FRACTURE.

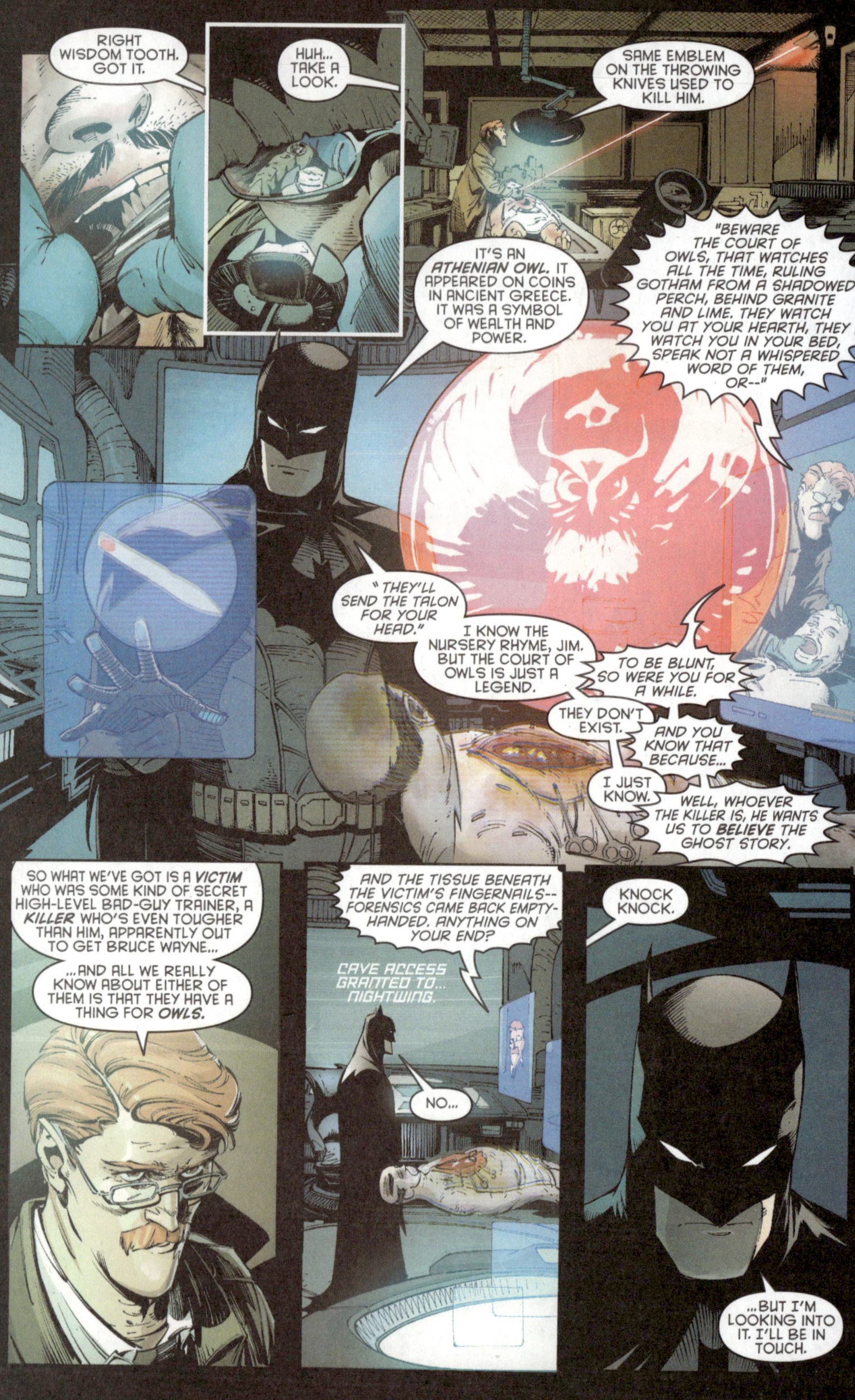
RIGHT WISDOM TOOTH. GOT IT.
HUH... TAKE A LOOK.
SAME EMBLEM ON THE THROWING KNIVES USED TO KILL HIM.
IT'S AN ATHENIAN OWL. IT APPEARED ON COINS IN ANCIENT GREECE. IT WAS A SYMBOL OF WEALTH AND POWER.
"BEWARE THE COURT OF OWLS, THAT WATCHES ALL THE TIME, RULING GOTHAM FROM A SHADOWED PERCH, BEHIND GRANITE AND LIME. THEY WATCH YOU AT YOUR HEARTH, THEY WATCH YOU IN YOUR BED, SPEAK NOT A WHISPERED WORD OF THEM, OR--"
"THEY'LL SEND THE TALON FOR YOUR HEAD."
I KNOW THE NURSERY RHYME, JIM. BUT THE COURT OF OWLS IS JUST A LEGEND.
TO BE BLUNT, SO WERE YOU FOR A WHILE.
THEY DON'T EXIST.
AND YOU KNOW THAT BECAUSE...
I JUST KNOW.
WELL, WHOEVER THE KILLER IS, HE WANTS US TO BELIEVE THE GHOST STORY.
SO WHAT WE'VE GOT IS A VICTIM WHO WAS SOME KIND OF SECRET HIGH-LEVEL BAD-GUY TRAINER, A KILLER WHO'S EVEN TOUGHER THAN HIM, APPARENTLY OUT TO GET BRUCE WAYNE...
...AND ALL WE REALLY KNOW ABOUT EITHER OF THEM IS THAT THEY HAVE A THING FOR OWLS.
AND THE TISSUE BENEATH THE VICTIM'S FINGERNAILS-- FORENSICS CAME BACK EMPTY-HANDED. ANYTHING ON YOUR END?
CAVE ACCESS GRANTED TO... NIGHTWING.
NO...
KNOCK KNOCK.
...BUT I'M LOOKING INTO IT. I'LL BE IN TOUCH.

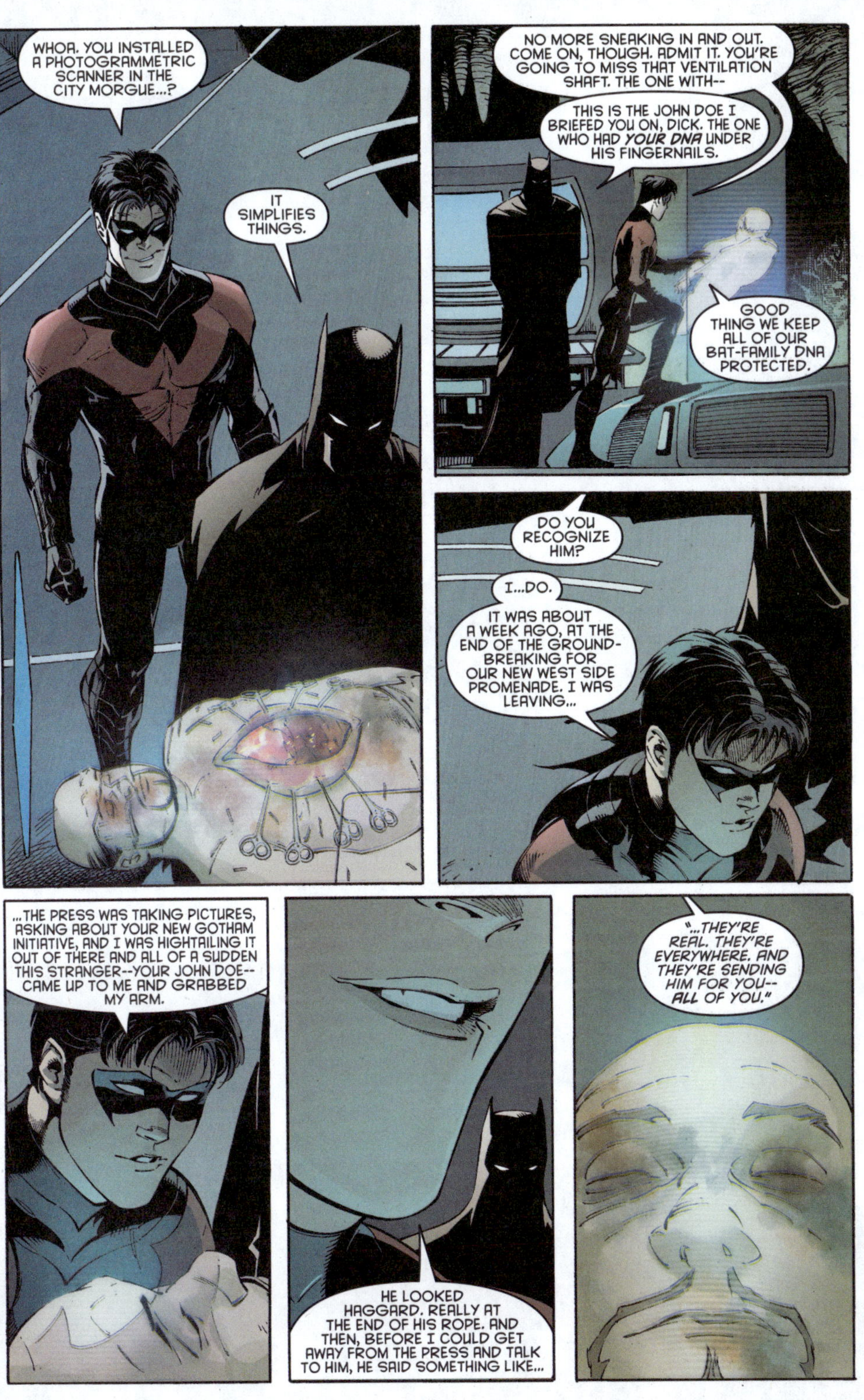
WHOA. YOU INSTALLED A PHOTOGRAMMETRIC SCANNER IN THE CITY MORGUE...?
IT SIMPLIFIES THINGS.
NO MORE SNEAKING IN AND OUT. COME ON, THOUGH. ADMIT IT. YOU'RE GOING TO MISS THAT VENTILATION SHAFT. THE ONE WITH--
THIS IS THE JOHN DOE I BRIEFED YOU ON, DICK. THE ONE WHO HAD *YOUR DNA* UNDER HIS FINGERNAILS.
GOOD THING WE KEEP ALL OF OUR BAT-FAMILY DNA PROTECTED.
DO YOU RECOGNIZE HIM?
I...DO.
IT WAS ABOUT A WEEK AGO, AT THE END OF THE GROUND-BREAKING FOR OUR NEW WEST SIDE PROMENADE. I WAS LEAVING...
...THE PRESS WAS TAKING PICTURES, ASKING ABOUT YOUR NEW GOTHAM INITIATIVE, AND I WAS HIGHTAILING IT OUT OF THERE AND ALL OF A SUDDEN THIS STRANGER--YOUR JOHN DOE--CAME UP TO ME AND GRABBED MY ARM.
HE LOOKED HAGGARD. REALLY AT THE END OF HIS ROPE. AND THEN, BEFORE I COULD GET AWAY FROM THE PRESS AND TALK TO HIM, HE SAID SOMETHING LIKE...
"...THEY'RE REAL. THEY'RE EVERYWHERE. AND THEY'RE SENDING HIM FOR YOU--*ALL* OF YOU."

AND THEN--
AND THEN SECURITY GOT TO HIM. BEFORE I COULD FOLLOW UP, HE WAS GONE. I NOTED IT, BUT HONESTLY, I JUST ASSUMED BY THE LOOKS OF HIM HE WAS A ZEALOT OR SOME-THING. ALL FIRE AND BRIMSTONE...
NOW, THOUGH... STILL, I DON'T GET WHY HE WOULD APPROACH ME WHEN YOU WERE THE ONE IN DANGER.
AND YOUR DNA.
WHEN SECURITY PULLED HIM OFF, HE STILL HAD MY ARM.
I CAN TAKE OFF MY GLOVE AND SHOW YOU. IT WAS A WEEK AGO, BUT THE SCRATCH MARKS ARE STILL THERE.
THERE'S NO NEED FOR THAT.
WELL, WELL. LOOK AT THIS.
I'LL LET YOU KNOW IF THERE ARE ANY MORE DEVELOPMENTS THAT PERTAIN TO YOU.
YOU ALREADY CHECKED THE SURVEILLANCE FOOTAGE FROM THE GROUNDBREAKING, DIDN'T YOU? THAT'S WHY YOU DON'T CARE ABOUT CHECKING MY ALIBI.
DICK, YOU KNOW ME BETTER THAN ANYONE, EXCEPT PERHAPS FOR ALFRED...
OF COURSE I CHECKED THE SURVEILLANCE FOOTAGE.
I HAVE TO GO.
WELL, ENJOY YOURSELF, PARTNER. BECAUSE ACCORDING TO YOUR JOHN DOE'S FLAMING NOTE...

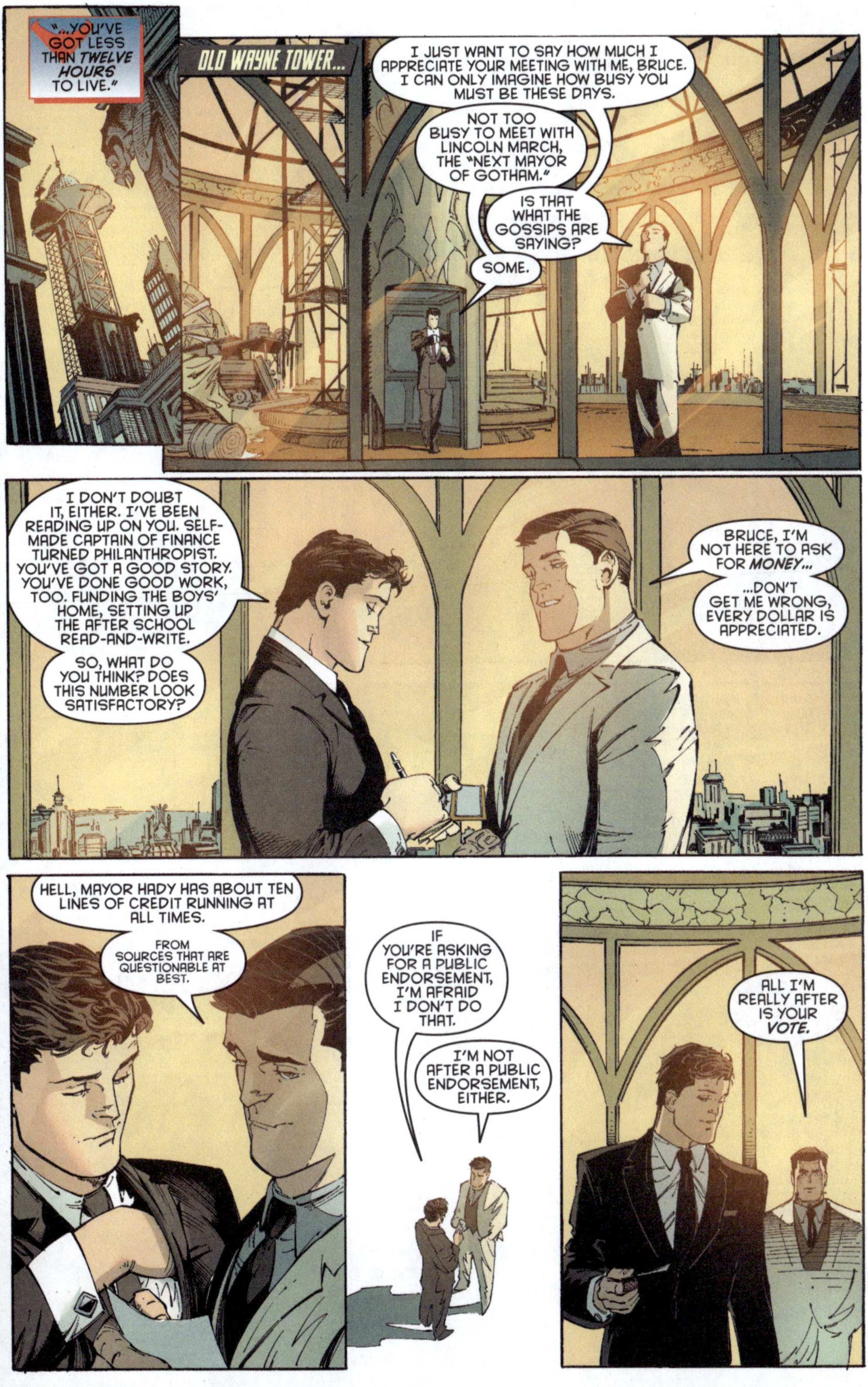

"...YOU'VE GOT LESS THAN TWELVE HOURS TO LIVE."
OLD WAYNE TOWER...
I JUST WANT TO SAY HOW MUCH I APPRECIATE YOUR MEETING WITH ME, BRUCE. I CAN ONLY IMAGINE HOW BUSY YOU MUST BE THESE DAYS.
NOT TOO BUSY TO MEET WITH LINCOLN MARCH, THE "NEXT MAYOR OF GOTHAM."
IS THAT WHAT THE GOSSIPS ARE SAYING?
SOME.
I DON'T DOUBT IT, EITHER. I'VE BEEN READING UP ON YOU. SELF-MADE CAPTAIN OF FINANCE TURNED PHILANTHROPIST. YOU'VE GOT A GOOD STORY. YOU'VE DONE GOOD WORK, TOO. FUNDING THE BOYS' HOME, SETTING UP THE AFTER SCHOOL READ-AND-WRITE.
SO, WHAT DO YOU THINK? DOES THIS NUMBER LOOK SATISFACTORY?
BRUCE, I'M NOT HERE TO ASK FOR MONEY...
...DON'T GET ME WRONG, EVERY DOLLAR IS APPRECIATED.
HELL, MAYOR HADY HAS ABOUT TEN LINES OF CREDIT RUNNING AT ALL TIMES.
FROM SOURCES THAT ARE QUESTIONABLE AT BEST.
IF YOU'RE ASKING FOR A PUBLIC ENDORSEMENT, I'M AFRAID I DON'T DO THAT.
I'M NOT AFTER A PUBLIC ENDORSEMENT, EITHER.
ALL I'M REALLY AFTER IS YOUR VOTE.

MY VOTE... YOU'VE COME A LONG WAY FOR ONE VOTE, LINCOLN.
THAT'S TRUE. BUT I BELIEVE IN WHAT YOU'RE DOING, BRUCE. THIS INITIATIVE TO REBUILD GOTHAM. IT'S A GOOD THING. AND TO BE FRANK, I SEE A FRIEND IN YOU.
A CYNIC WOULD SAY YOU SEE AN OPPORTUNITY.
THAT'S TRUE. AND A CYNIC WOULD SAY YOU'RE SPEARHEADING THIS NEW GOTHAM INITIATIVE FOR THE IMAGE OF YOUR COMPANY. BECAUSE IT'S A PUBLIC HOLDING, AND SO ON. FOR PRIVATE PURPOSES.
IS THAT WHAT THE GOSSIPS SAY?
SOME.
MAYBE THEY'RE RIGHT.
I SHOULD BE GOING. I'LL LEAVE THE CHECK ON THE TABLE.
YOU KNOW, BRUCE, I LOST MY PARENTS WHEN I WAS A BOY, TOO.
IT'S STRANGE, ISN'T IT? THE WAY IT'S JUST THE DETAILS... THE DETAILS THAT STAY WITH YOU? I CAN BARELY REMEMBER MY MOTHER'S FACE ANYMORE.
BUT I REMEMBER THIS *PIN*--CLEAR AS DAY--THIS PIN SHE WAS WEARING THE DAY OF THE ACCIDENT. I'D MADE IT FOR HER AT SCHOOL IN CERAMICS. IT WAS THIS LITTLE HEART, BUT IT WAS ALL LOPSIDED--WITH ONE SIDE BIGGER THAN THE OTHER.
SHE WAS WEARING IT PINNED TO THIS FANCY DRESS OF HERS. MY LITTLE UGLY PIN. I DON'T REMEMBER THE DRUNK DRIVER HITTING US. I DON'T REMEMBER MUCH OF THE ACCIDENT...
*I DO* REMEMBER SEEING THE PIN ON THE GROUND THOUGH, AS THE PARAMEDICS TOOK ME AWAY. THE PIN, PERFECTLY PRESERVED, NOT CRACKED OR BROKEN. JUST LYING IN THE ROAD. ALL I WANTED WAS FOR SOMEONE TO PICK IT UP.

I LOST EVERYTHING I HAD THAT NIGHT. FOR A LONG TIME AFTER, I LIVED IN A STATE OF TOTAL *HOPELESSNESS.* I HATED THE WORLD.
BUT THEN I GOT FUNDING FOR SCHOOL. I WAS ABLE TO GO TO CITY COLLEGE. THE CITY SAVED ME, BRUCE. *GOTHAM* SAVED ME.
IT GAVE ME A PURPOSE WHEN I WAS ALONE. JUST LIKE I'LL BET IT DID FOR *YOU.*
WHEN I LOOK AT YOU, I SEE AN ALLY. A *REAL* ONE. AND AS I'M SURE YOU KNOW, THIS IS A CITY WHERE ALLIES ARE FEW AND FAR BETWEEN.
ESPECIALLY *NOW.*
"ESPECIALLY NOW," WHY?
SOMETHING BAD HAS COME BACK TO GOTHAM, BRUCE. SOMETHING ANCIENT AND POWERFUL... AND *EVIL.*
LINCOLN, WHAT ARE YOU TALKING--

CRASH
WHAT THE--
YOU... IF YOU THINK YOU CAN SCARE--
UNH!
THUCK
LINCOLN!

Don't recognize him.
Just me and him, but still... have to be careful. Restrain myself. Never know who's watching.
Someone new.
Someone fast.
Go for strikes that look like lucky blows.
Solar plexus.
Mandibular nerv--
All right. Playtime's over.

Doesn't make sense. It only takes eleven pounds of pressure to collapse a windpipe.
I'm applying over one hundred and he's not even flinching.
Must be on something.
Some kind of venom?
BRUCE WAYNE. THE COURT OF OWLS HAS SENTENCED YOU TO DIE.

Too far out to grab for the ring of seven...
...by the time I reach the other five guardians I'll be at terminal velocity.
The force will rip my arms off.
HOW I LOVE KILLING WAYNES.

There's something I didn't mention earlier, about the design of Old Wayne Tower.
Something your tour guide wouldn't mention, either. Because there's one guardian people don't tell you about, when you visit.
They don't bother to mention it because it was added later, in 1930, and because it sits in the middle of the building and can't be seen from the elevators or the deck.
The **thirteenth guardian.** Installed by Alan's son, Henry, my great-grandfather.
The guardian for visitors to Gotham arriving by air.

Whoever it was that just tried to kill me, he was good.
But he made one mistake.
He tried to use Gotham's legends against me.
CCPD
CCPD
EMT
But I'm the only legend this city needs.

In many ways, it's my oldest and truest friend.
And it knows me better than anyone, just as I know it.
Which is why I can say that there is no Court of Owls.
Not in Gotham.
Not in my city.

Capullo
'11
+fco

# CHAPTER THREE • THE THIRTEENTH HOUR

HELP!
GOTHAM CITY. WINTER, 1922
SOMEONE HELP ME!
THEY'RE... COMING FOR ME!
HONK
SREEECH
HELP! PLEASE!
HEY THERE, PAL, YOU CAN'T--
PSST... JIMMY.
DON'T YOU *RECOGNIZE* HIM?
IT'S *ALAN WAYNE.* THE GUY BUILT HALF THIS CITY. GEEZ, GET HIM A BLANKET, WILL YOU, BEFORE HE FREEZES.

THEY'RE AFTER ME! PLEASE!
IT'S OKAY, MR. WAYNE. WE'RE HERE. NOW... WHO'S AFTER YOU?
THEY'RE EVERYWHERE, DON'T YOU SEE? THE THIRTEENTH HOUR, IT'S UPON US! THEY'RE COMING!
AND THEIR NESTS-- THEIR NESTS ARE ALL AROUND! THEY'RE IN MY HOME! MY HOME! PLEASE!
WHAT SHOULD WE DO? GET THE PADDY?
THE PADDY...WHAT ARE YOU, CRAZY? THE PRESS WOULD DRAG THE POOR GUY DOWN INTO--
AIIIEEEE!
THERE! THE MANHOLE!
DID HE FALL OR JUMP?
I DIDN'T SEE!
MR. WAYNE! MR. WAYNE! ARE YOU DOWN THERE?!

OKAY! OKAY!
I WILL TELL YOU WHERE HE WILL BE!
GOTHAM CITY. NOW...
TALK.
YOU SAY YOU ARE LOOKING FOR A MAN IN A DARK COSTUME, AN ENFORCER WITH A MASK TO HIDE HIS FACE. I WILL TELL YOU THAT TOMORROW...
...HEH HEH... THERE WILL BE ONE AT THE MORGUE!
The man making the questionable jokes is named Luka Volk.
He's the "pakhan" of a Gotham branch of the Ukrainian mob.

They call themselves "Whisper Gang."
And they're one of five gangs that control smuggling in and out of Gotham by rail.
Two days ago, an assassin dressed like an owl tried to kill me while I was meeting with a local politician.
With no security footage of the assassin coming or going from Old Wayne Tower, my assumption is that he came in through the rail lines that converge beneath the building...
...then found a way up through the service elevators. Which means one of the rail gangs saw him and took some toll from him.
The gangs have divided the lines among them.
One line for each gang. One is Yakuza. One is La Eme. Five rail lines. Five gangs.

I've already chatted with the other four gangs.
Whisper Gang is known to be the most vicious and brutal of the five, though.
The candidates--or "sixths"--are given extensive weapons training overseas, before being allowed to travel to the States.
Once here, they're each fitted with an iron mask, symbolic of their loyalty to the gang. A muzzle to prove they'll never "snitch."
1
The mask is soldered together at the back of the head, and can't be removed for at least a year, until the sixth has proven himself.
All of which makes them pretty tough...

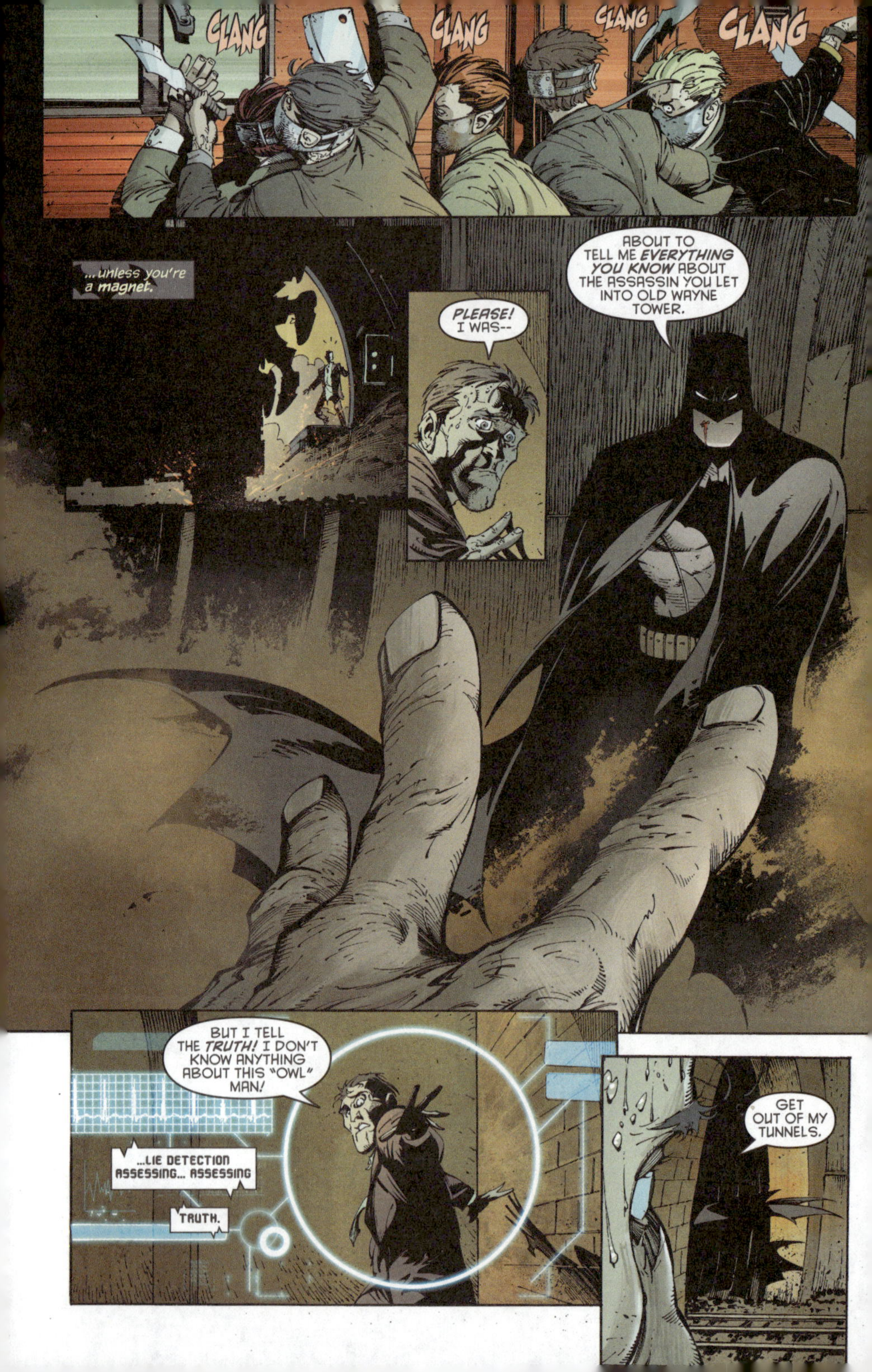
CLANG
CLANG
CLANG
CLANG
...unless you're a magnet.
PLEASE! I WAS--
ABOUT TO TELL ME EVERYTHING YOU KNOW ABOUT THE ASSASSIN YOU LET INTO OLD WAYNE TOWER.
BUT I TELL THE TRUTH! I DON'T KNOW ANYTHING ABOUT THIS "OWL" MAN!
...LIE DETECTION ASSESSING... ASSESSING
TRUTH.
GET OUT OF MY TUNNELS.

SECOND MATRIX READY FOR VOICE ANALYSIS.
LAUNCH VOICE ANALYSIS.
NOW LET'S SEE WHO YOU ARE.
"BRUCE WAYNE. THE COURT OF OWLS HAS SENTENCED YOU TO DIE."
SEARCHING, SEARCHING... VOICE ANALYSIS: SEARCH FAILED.
DAMN. RUN AGAIN.
I'LL LEAVE THIS IN ARM'S REACH, SIR.
IF I MAY, THOUGH. THE MORNING BEFORE LAST, I CAME ACROSS AN ARTICLE IN THE SCIENCES PORTION OF THE GAZETTE.
IT APPEARS THAT RESEARCHERS IN GERMANY-- ORNITHOLOGISTS-- RECENTLY DISCOVERED THAT MOST BATS DEPEND ON THE SUNSET FOR LONG-DISTANCE NAVIGATION.
WHICH IS TO SAY THEY NEED TO EXPERIENCE TWILIGHT IN ORDER TO CALIBRATE THEIR INTERNAL COMPASS.
IN OTHER WORDS, MASTER BRUCE, BATS NEED A LITTLE SUNLIGHT ONCE IN A WHILE TO FLY STRAIGHT, IF YOU WILL.
I KNOW PLENTY ABOUT BATS, ALFRED. TELL ME WHAT YOU KNOW ABOUT OWLS.
SIR?

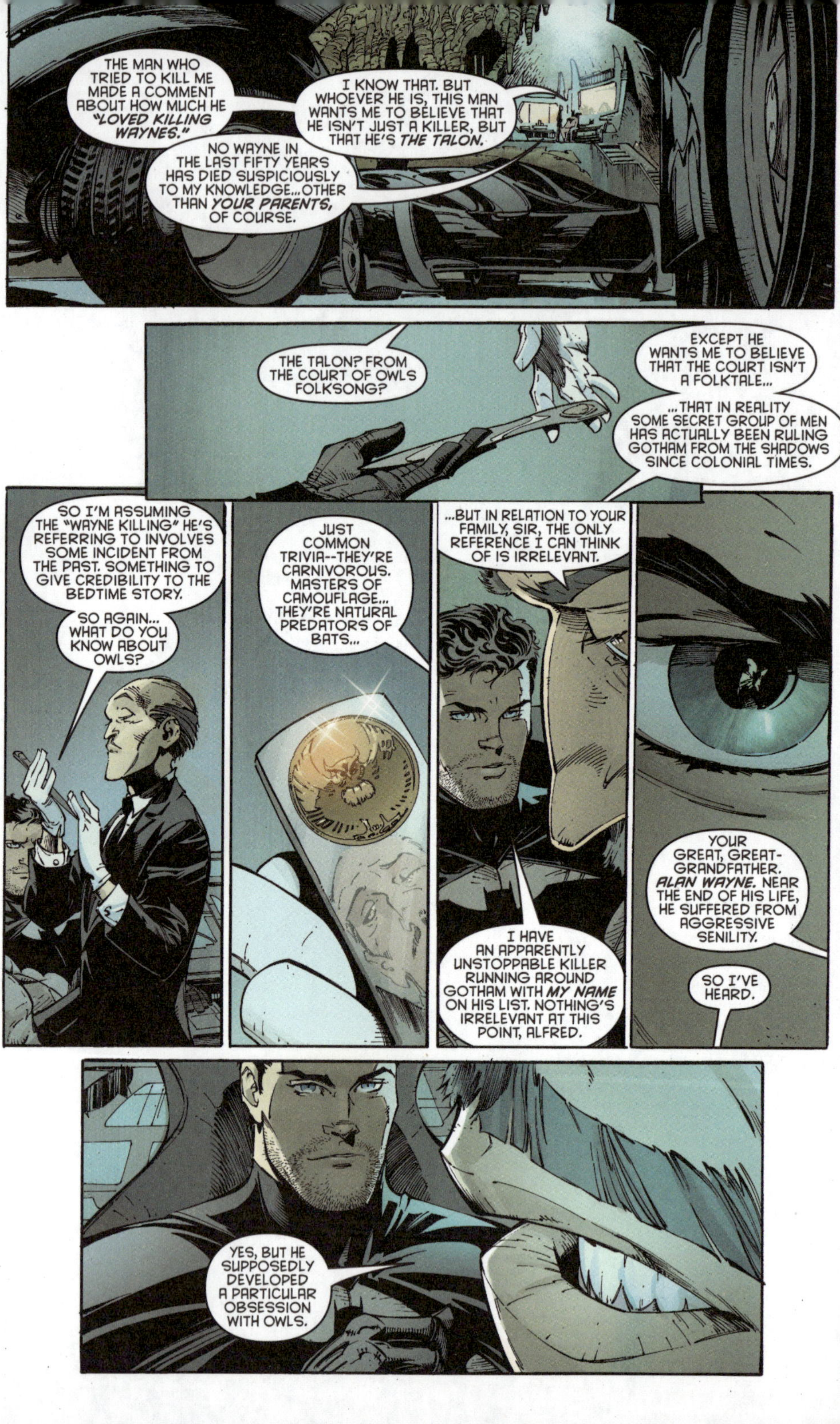
THE MAN WHO TRIED TO KILL ME MADE A COMMENT ABOUT HOW MUCH HE "LOVED KILLING WAYNES."
NO WAYNE IN THE LAST FIFTY YEARS HAS DIED SUSPICIOUSLY TO MY KNOWLEDGE...OTHER THAN YOUR PARENTS, OF COURSE.
I KNOW THAT. BUT WHOEVER HE IS, THIS MAN WANTS ME TO BELIEVE THAT HE ISN'T JUST A KILLER, BUT THAT HE'S THE TALON.
THE TALON? FROM THE COURT OF OWLS FOLKSONG?
EXCEPT HE WANTS ME TO BELIEVE THAT THE COURT ISN'T A FOLKTALE...
...THAT IN REALITY SOME SECRET GROUP OF MEN HAS ACTUALLY BEEN RULING GOTHAM FROM THE SHADOWS SINCE COLONIAL TIMES.
SO I'M ASSUMING THE "WAYNE KILLING" HE'S REFERRING TO INVOLVES SOME INCIDENT FROM THE PAST. SOMETHING TO GIVE CREDIBILITY TO THE BEDTIME STORY.
SO AGAIN... WHAT DO YOU KNOW ABOUT OWLS?
JUST COMMON TRIVIA--THEY'RE CARNIVOROUS. MASTERS OF CAMOUFLAGE... THEY'RE NATURAL PREDATORS OF BATS...
...BUT IN RELATION TO YOUR FAMILY, SIR, THE ONLY REFERENCE I CAN THINK OF IS IRRELEVANT.
I HAVE AN APPARENTLY UNSTOPPABLE KILLER RUNNING AROUND GOTHAM WITH MY NAME ON HIS LIST. NOTHING'S IRRELEVANT AT THIS POINT, ALFRED.
YOUR GREAT, GREAT-GRANDFATHER. ALAN WAYNE. NEAR THE END OF HIS LIFE, HE SUFFERED FROM AGGRESSIVE SENILITY.
SO I'VE HEARD.
YES, BUT HE SUPPOSEDLY DEVELOPED A PARTICULAR OBSESSION WITH OWLS.

HE SUFFERED FROM A SEVERE PARANOIA ABOUT THE BIRDS, SOME OBSESSION WITH THE IDEA THAT THEY WERE CONSPIRING AGAINST HIM.
TO HEAR MY FATHER TELL IT, MASTER ALAN BOARDED UP HIS WINDOWS FOR FEAR THAT ONE NIGHT THE OWLS WOULD COME FOR HIM.
BUT EVEN THIS DIDN'T HELP, AS HE SOON BECAME GRIPPED BY THE NOTION THAT THEY--THE OWLS-- WERE ROOSTING INSIDE HIS HOME. IN THE WALLS.
IF YOU LOOK AT HIS LAST PORTRAIT IN THE GALLERY, AT THE BUILDINGS HE DESIGNED, FEATURED IN THE BACKGROUND, YOU'LL NOTICE OWLS PERCHED ALONG THE MOLDINGS.
BUT HIS DEATH...
NO, YOU'RE CORRECT. HE DROWNED, HAVING FALLEN INTO AN OPEN MANHOLE IN THE GOTHAM SEWER. NO FOUL PLAY WAS SUSPECTED.
I'VE TAKEN THE LIBERTY OF PREPARING YOU SOME BLACK TEA WITH MEDICINAL--
NO TIME, ALFRED. I'M ON MY WAY OUT.
MAY I SUGGEST YOU TAKE THE DAY TO REST, SIR. WITH THE INJURIES YOU SUSTAINED IN THE FALL, AND THE STAB WOUNDS--
YOU SAID IT YOURSELF, ALFRED...

"...EVEN BATS NEED SUNSHINE."
GOTHAM GENERAL HOSPITAL
YOU'RE MAKING ME LOOK BAD, BRUCE.
AFTER ALL, I TOOK ONE KNIFE...YOU TOOK TWO AND GOT KICKED OUT A THIRTY-STORY WINDOW.
BUT I'M THE ONE IN BED, EATING JELLO IN A BUTTLESS NIGHTGOWN. GOOD THING YOU'RE NOT RUNNING AGAINST ME.
ACTUALLY, LINCOLN, I AM. THAT'S WHAT I CAME TO TELL YOU.
HEH -KOFF KOFF- DON'T MAKE ME LAUGH.
ACTUALLY, I WANTED TO SPEAK WITH YOU PRIVATELY. JUST BEFORE THAT ATTACKER CAME IN, YOU WERE TALKING ABOUT SOMETHING BAD HAVING RETURNED TO GOTHAM.
YES -KOFF-
I'D BEEN GETTING WARNINGS, BRUCE. WHISPERS FROM PEOPLE TO DROP MY BID FOR MAYOR.
AND THEN, TWO WEEKS AGO, I WOKE TO FIND AN OWL IN MY APARTMENT.
JUST PERCHED THERE IN MY CLOSET. A LITTLE PILE OF BONES BENEATH IT.

STILL, I DIDN'T REALLY BELIEVE IT WAS THEM BEHIND THE THREATS. THAT IT *COULD* BE THEM.
BUT IT SCARED ME ENOUGH THAT I ASKED MY FRIENDS AT THE G.C.P.D. TO KEEP A BEAD ON ANYTHING RELATED. SO WHEN THE REPORT CAME IN ABOUT YOU BEING TARGETED BY THEM, TOO--ABOUT HOW THAT MAN LEFT YOU A MESSAGE...THAT JOHN DOE KILLED BY THE TALON--
THE VERDICT ON WHO KILLED THAT MAN IS STILL OUT.
BEWARE THE COURT OF OWLS, BRUCE, THAT WATCHES ALL THE TIME. RULING GOTHAM FROM SHADOWED PERCH, BEHIND GRANITE AND LIME. THEY WATCH YOU AT YOUR HEARTH, THEY WATCH YOU IN YOUR...
...YOUR BED.
SPEAK NOT A WHISPERED WORD OF THEM, OR THEY'LL SEND THE TALON--
I'VE BEEN HEARING THAT OLD RHYME A LOT LATELY, LINCOLN. FRANKLY, I'M GETTING TIRED OF IT.
NOW, IF THERE REALLY *WAS* A COURT OF OWLS...
...DON'T YOU THINK, WITH MY ROOTS IN THIS CITY, I'D HAVE LEARNED THEY WERE REAL LONG AGO?
UNLESS...
UNLESS WHAT?
UNLESS THEY DIDN'T WANT YOU TO. UNTIL NOW.
MAYBE THIS NEW GOTHAM INITIATIVE OF YOURS, RESHAPING THE CITY, MAYBE THEY'RE JUST NOW PAYING ATTENTION TO YOU, TOO. SAME WITH ME.

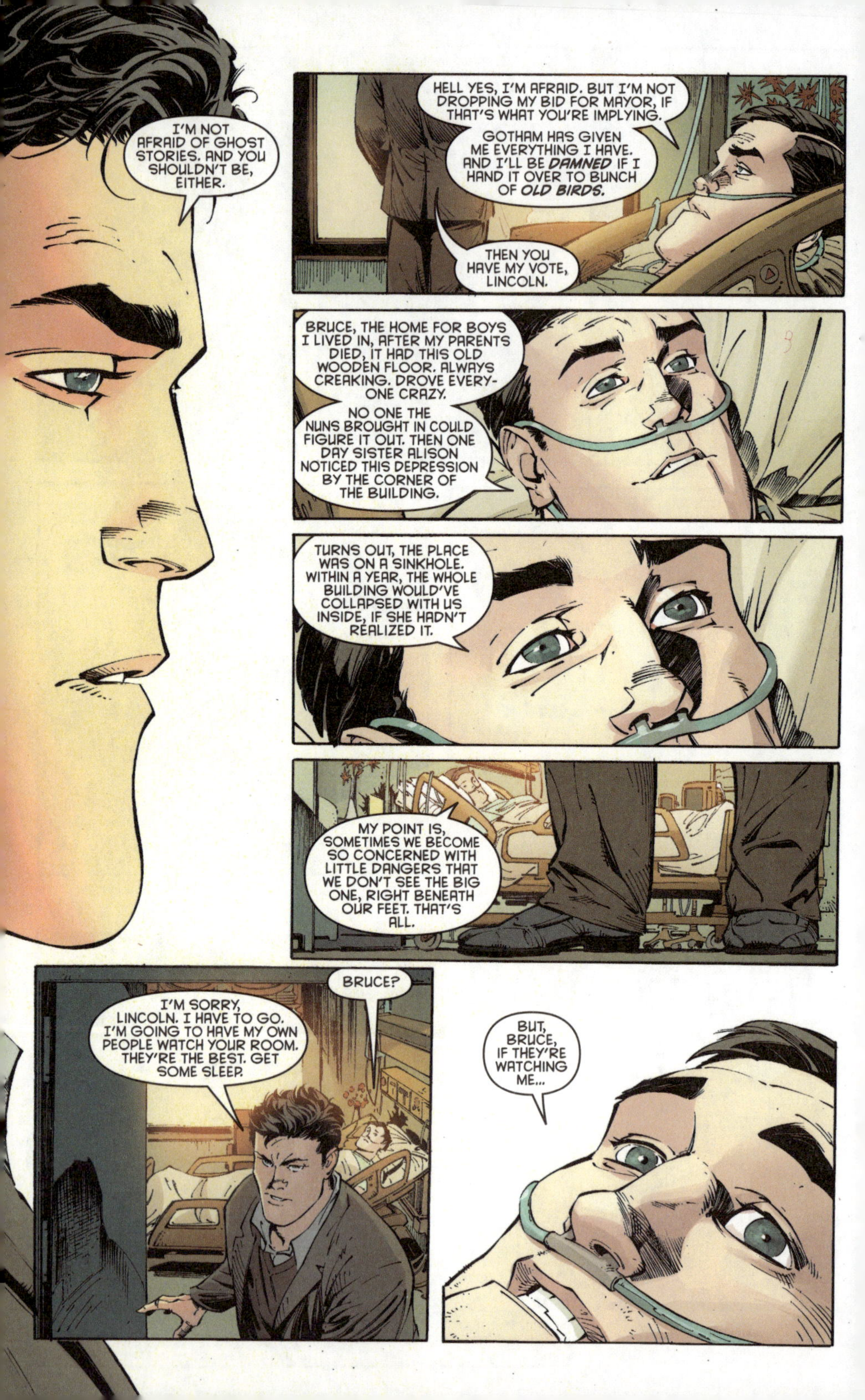
I'M NOT AFRAID OF GHOST STORIES. AND YOU SHOULDN'T BE, EITHER.
HELL YES, I'M AFRAID. BUT I'M NOT DROPPING MY BID FOR MAYOR, IF THAT'S WHAT YOU'RE IMPLYING.
GOTHAM HAS GIVEN ME EVERYTHING I HAVE. AND I'LL BE DAMNED IF I HAND IT OVER TO BUNCH OF OLD BIRDS.
THEN YOU HAVE MY VOTE, LINCOLN.
BRUCE, THE HOME FOR BOYS I LIVED IN, AFTER MY PARENTS DIED, IT HAD THIS OLD WOODEN FLOOR. ALWAYS CREAKING. DROVE EVERY-ONE CRAZY.
NO ONE THE NUNS BROUGHT IN COULD FIGURE IT OUT. THEN ONE DAY SISTER ALISON NOTICED THIS DEPRESSION BY THE CORNER OF THE BUILDING.
TURNS OUT, THE PLACE WAS ON A SINKHOLE. WITHIN A YEAR, THE WHOLE BUILDING WOULD'VE COLLAPSED WITH US INSIDE, IF SHE HADN'T REALIZED IT.
MY POINT IS, SOMETIMES WE BECOME SO CONCERNED WITH LITTLE DANGERS THAT WE DON'T SEE THE BIG ONE, RIGHT BENEATH OUR FEET. THAT'S ALL.
I'M SORRY, LINCOLN. I HAVE TO GO. I'M GOING TO HAVE MY OWN PEOPLE WATCH YOUR ROOM. THEY'RE THE BEST. GET SOME SLEEP.
BRUCE?
BUT, BRUCE, IF THEY'RE WATCHING ME...

"...WHO'S WATCHING YOU?"
Historically, cities are places of superstition.
After all, people come to them from all over the world, from small towns and villages, places they've lived for generations, to inhabit giant mazes of glass and steel, shadow and merciless light.
They'd cling to beliefs from home about what keeps you safe, and what to avoid.
A black cat crosses your path, you'll be plagued by bad luck.
A thirteenth guest at dinner means someone in the party will die at midnight.
My great-grandfather, Alan Wayne, understood the power of superstition. As such, he was one of the first men to eliminate a thirteenth floor from his buildings.
Funny thing, though. To really make good on the superstition, you were supposed to leave a small space in the building between floors twelve and fourteen, a false floor, to contain the bad luck of number thirteen.
A space sealed off from the world, inaccessible. Just a blank slot in the building. An absence like a breath held when passing a graveyard.
A space just big enough--in theory--for a man to hide in. Perhaps a killer dressed like an owl.

And on the subject of owls, here's a fact about them.
They're one of the rare birds that doesn't build its own nest.
Instead, what they do is find nests abandoned or in use by rival birds and **take them over.**
In essence, they invade an enemy's territory...

...and build their nests inside his home.
BINGO.

JUNE, 1891
ALFRED.
SIR?
THE FUND ESTABLISHED IN ALAN WAYNE'S NAME.

"IT STILL EXISTS, DOESN'T IT?"
THE ALAN WAYNE TRUST FOR ASSISTING YOUNG ARCHITECTS. IT'S A FUND TO BE USED FOR PROGRESSIVE ADDITIONS TO GOTHAM'S SKYLINE.
"PULL UP THE ADDRESSES OF ALL THE BUILDINGS FUNDED BY THAT TRUST OVER THE LAST CENTURY AND A HALF."
I'M UPLOADING THE ADDRESSES NOW.
THERE ARE NEARLY TWENTY BUILDINGS IN ALL, ROUGHLY ONE EVERY DECADE FOR THE LAST HUNDRED AND FIFTY YEARS...

...THE MOST RECENT WAS BUILT JUST FIVE YEARS AGO.
JUNE 1963

ALFRED. I WANT YOU TO OPEN ALAN WAYNE'S CRYPT.
SIR?
HE WAS RIGHT.
I DON'T UNDERSTAND.
ABOUT THE OWL NESTS.
WHAT ABOUT THEM? SIR?
THEY'RE IN OUR HOMES.
JUNE, 2006

ALL THIS TIME. RIGHT UNDER OUR FE--
SIR?
KRABOOOOM

Capullo
'11
+fco

# CHAPTER FOUR • FACE THE COURT • PART ON

Most people assume the danger of a trip-wire lies in the blast.
KABOOOM

Not so.
UNNH!
The real threat from a tripwire comes later...
...in the aftermath.
The truth is, a trip-wire is a greater instrument of Fear than of violence.
It demoralizes and terrorizes everyone in range, suggesting that the enemy knows the terrain better than you do, that this is their home, and they're every-where at once...
...ready to bear down at any moment.
THUM

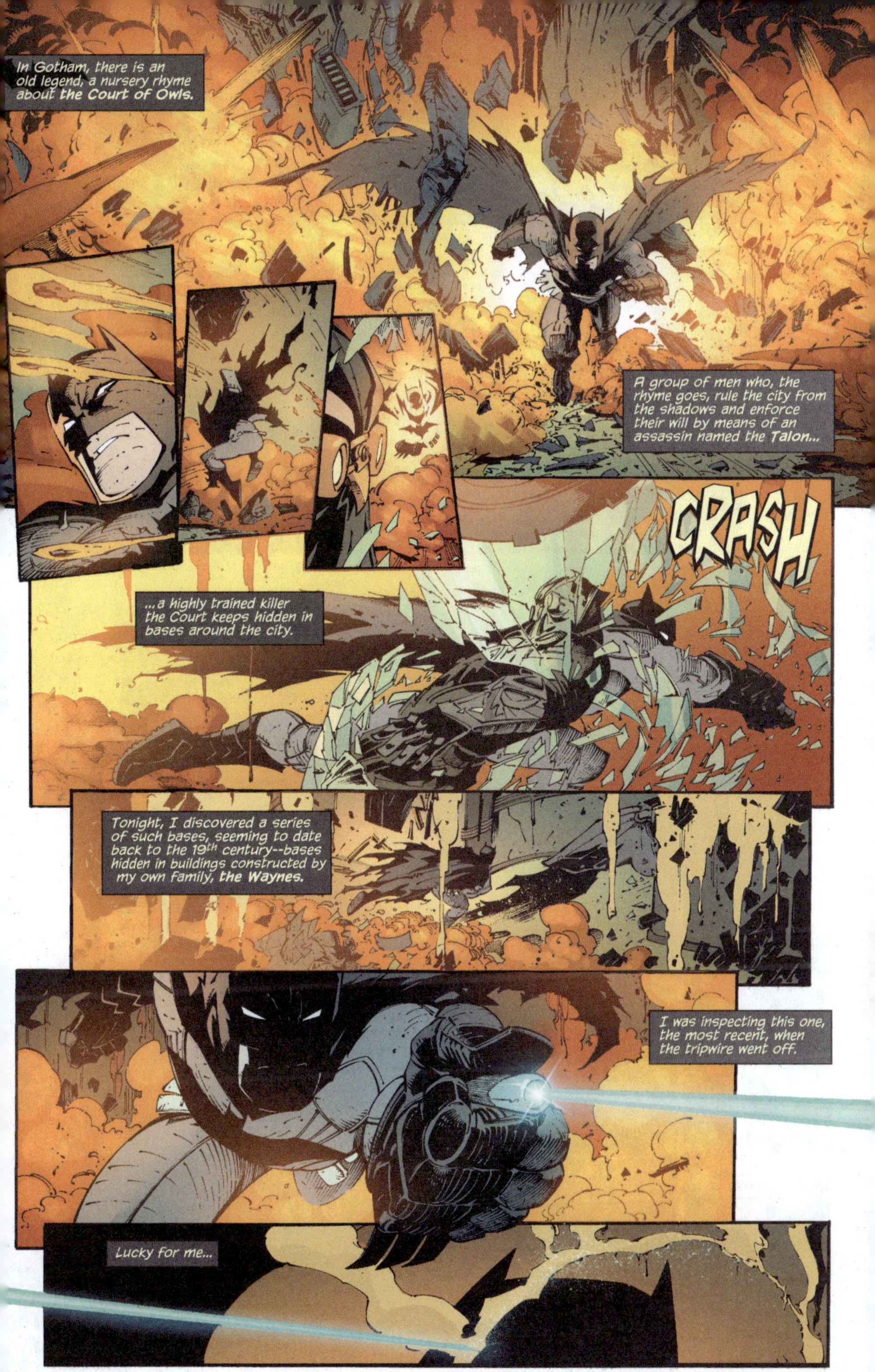

In Gotham, there is an old legend, a nursery rhyme about the Court of Owls.
A group of men who, the rhyme goes, rule the city from the shadows and enforce their will by means of an assassin named the Talon...
CRASH
...a highly trained killer the Court keeps hidden in bases around the city.
Tonight, I discovered a series of such bases, seeming to date back to the 19th century--bases hidden in buildings constructed by my own family, the Waynes.
I was inspecting this one, the most recent, when the tripwire went off.
Lucky for me...

...I don't scare easily.
"IF ALL THIS IS TRUE, THEN THE END--THE REAL END--IS NEAR..."

"...AND FRANKLY, I JUST CAN'T ACCEPT IT."
"TO BE FAIR, HE HAS TAKEN AN EXTRAORDINARY BIT OF PUNISHMENT OF LATE, MASTER RICHARD."
"BRUCE RESTING?"
"IT'S TRUE, SIR."
"AND HOW MANY DO YOU NEED TO SLIP HIM NOWADAYS...?"
"...ALFIE?"
"5 MILLIGRAMS."
"5 MILLIGRAMS OF ACE? THAT'D BRING DOWN A--"
"I'M AWARE OF THE EFFECTS, MASTER RICHARD. NOW, I'M AFRAID I MUST RETURN TO MY DUTIES. IF THERE'S NOTHING ELSE YOU NEED...?"
BRUCE? BRUCE, ARE YOU AWAKE?
AND ALL IS RIGHT IN THE WORLD.

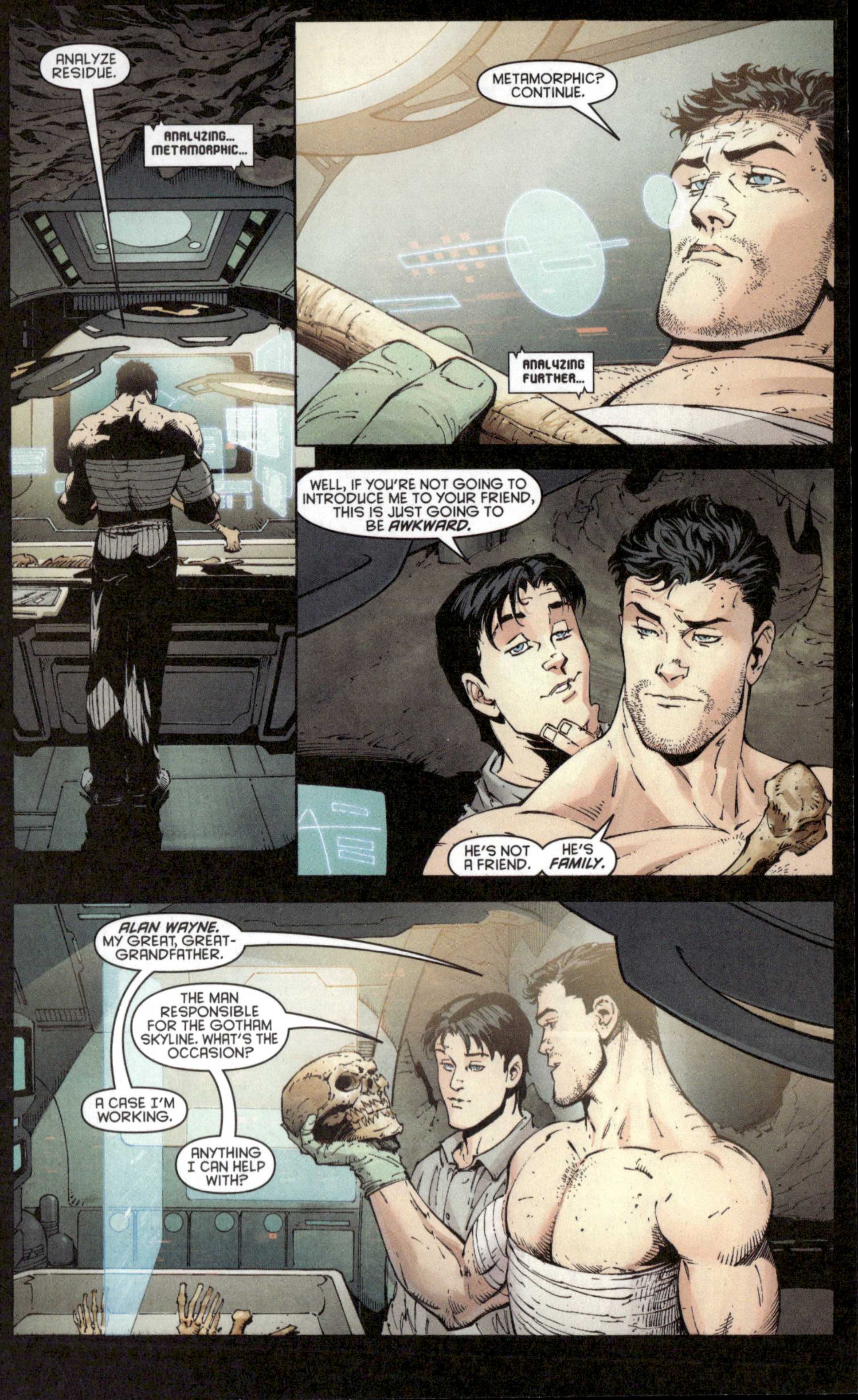

ANALYZE RESIDUE.
ANALYZING... METAMORPHIC...
METAMORPHIC? CONTINUE.
ANALYZING FURTHER...
WELL, IF YOU'RE NOT GOING TO INTRODUCE ME TO YOUR FRIEND, THIS IS JUST GOING TO BE *AWKWARD.*
HE'S NOT A FRIEND.
HE'S *FAMILY.*
*ALAN WAYNE.* MY GREAT, GREAT-GRANDFATHER.
THE MAN RESPONSIBLE FOR THE GOTHAM SKYLINE. WHAT'S THE OCCASION?
A CASE I'M WORKING.
ANYTHING I CAN HELP WITH?

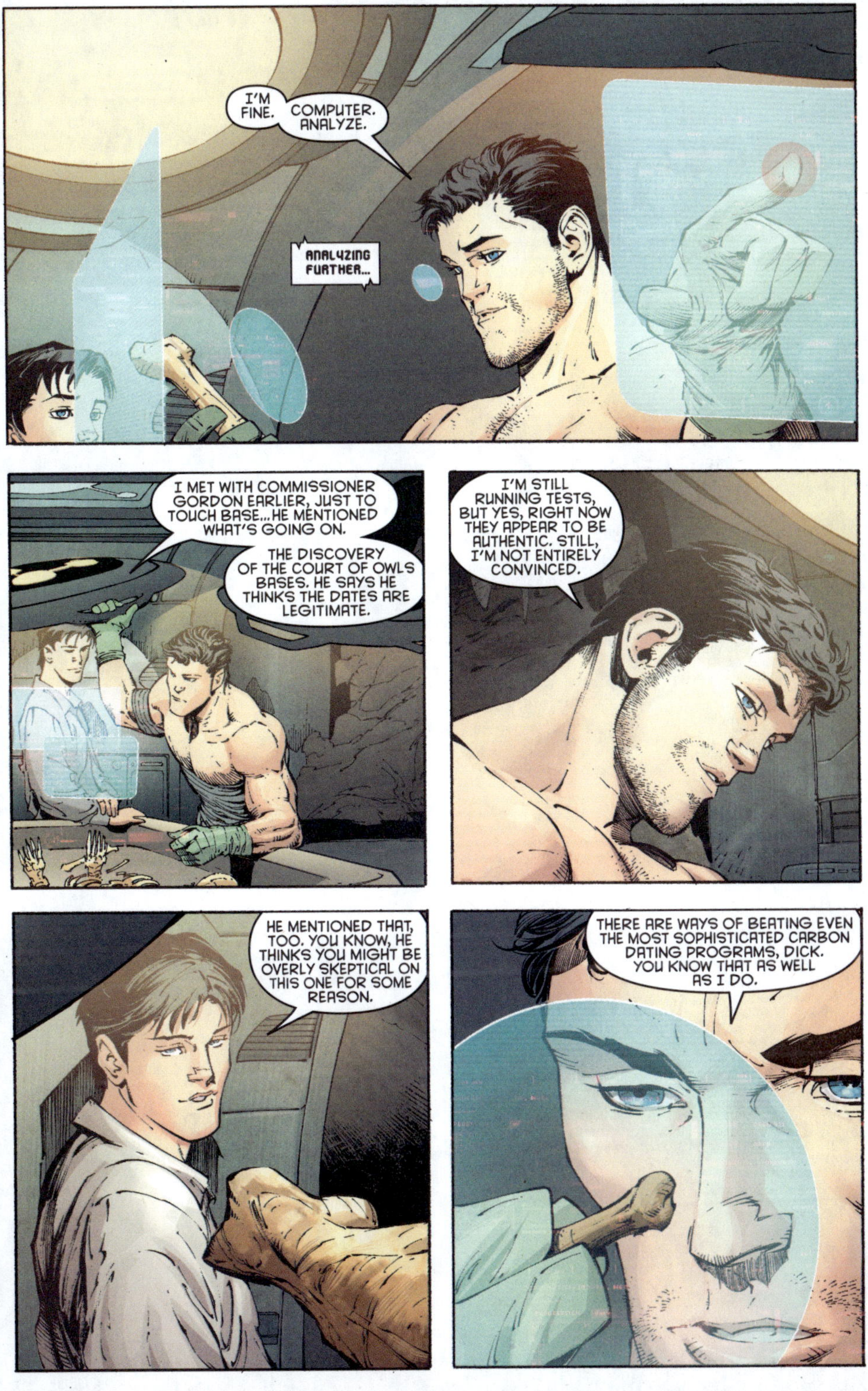
I'M FINE.
COMPUTER. ANALYZE.
ANALYZING FURTHER...
I MET WITH COMMISSIONER GORDON EARLIER, JUST TO TOUCH BASE...HE MENTIONED WHAT'S GOING ON.
THE DISCOVERY OF THE COURT OF OWLS BASES. HE SAYS HE THINKS THE DATES ARE LEGITIMATE.
I'M STILL RUNNING TESTS, BUT YES, RIGHT NOW THEY APPEAR TO BE AUTHENTIC. STILL, I'M NOT ENTIRELY CONVINCED.
HE MENTIONED THAT, TOO. YOU KNOW, HE THINKS YOU MIGHT BE OVERLY SKEPTICAL ON THIS ONE FOR SOME REASON.
THERE ARE WAYS OF BEATING EVEN THE MOST SOPHISTICATED CARBON DATING PROGRAMS, DICK. YOU KNOW THAT AS WELL AS I DO.

I DO...BUT I ALSO KNOW THAT YOU'RE BURNING IT AT BOTH ENDS ON THIS ONE. YOU'RE WORKING LIKE A MAN OBSESSED--OR MORE OBSESSED THAN USUAL--AND AS SUCH, IT'S POSSIBLE YOU'RE NOT SEEING THE FOREST FOR THE TREES.
ANALYSIS NEARLY COMPLETE...
CONTINUE.
THE POINT IS--
HOLD ON. I WAS TALKING TO THE COMPUTER.
COMPUTER--
BRUCE, WE'RE WORRIED ABOUT YOU, ALL RIGHT?
TWICE THIS MONTH YOU CAME CLOSE TO GETTING KILLED, AND SOME OF US THINK IT'S BECAUSE YOU'RE UNDERESTIMATING YOUR ENEMY HERE.
JIM SAID THAT?
YES, HE DID. THE JOHN DOE WHO CAME UP TO ME--A HIGHLY GHOSTED ID. HE'S KILLED BY AN ASSASSIN CALLING HIMSELF THE TALON.
YOU DROP THE GUY OFF A BUILDING AND HE GETS UP AND KILLS HIS RIDE TO THE MORGUE. NOW YOU DISCOVER THESE BASES, HIDDEN IN WAYNE BUILDINGS...
...BASES THAT SEEM TO BE FROM DIFFERENT DECADES DATING BACK TO THE 1800s. HOW CAN YOU NOT BE A LITTLE APPREHENSIVE ABOUT WHAT MIGHT BE ON THE OTHER SIDE OF THE EQUAL SIGN HERE?
I'M BEING OBJECTIVE, DICK. LIKE I TAUGHT YOU TO BE.
COMPUTER--RUN A SECONDARY TEST FOR SHALE.
RUNNING...
TAKE CARE, BRUCE. I HAVE A PLANE TO CATCH.

DICK...
THERE IS NO COURT OF OWLS. I KNOW BECAUSE I LOOKED INTO IT.
WHEN, BRUCE? I NEVER HEARD ABOUT IT, AND I WAS HERE FOR--
IT WAS BEFORE THAT. WHEN I WAS A BOY.
ANALYSIS COM--
SHUT UP.
PAUSING...
IT WAS AFTER MY PARENTS WERE KILLED.
IN THE WEEKS FOLLOWING THEIR MURDER...
"...I WAS...LOST.
"I COULDN'T ACCEPT IT."
"YOU WERE A KID, BRUCE. I WAS THE SAME. HOW ARE YOU SUPPOSED TO ACCEPT--"
"NO, DICK...
"...I COULDN'T ACCEPT THAT IT WAS RANDOM.
"THAT SOME PLAIN OLD JOE CHILL, SOME NO-NAME, HAD KILLED MY PARENTS OVER NOTHING BUT POCKET CHANGE AND PEARLS.
"DEEP DOWN I BELIEVED--I KNEW--THERE HAD TO BE SOMETHING BIGGER AT WORK."

"OF COURSE, GROWING UP, I'D HEARD THE OLD LEGEND OF THE COURT OF OWLS.
"I'D ASKED MY FATHER ABOUT THEM, BUT HE ALWAYS LAUGHED OFF THE IDEA.
"BUT EVEN SO, IN THE DAYS BEFORE MY PARENTS' DEATH, THERE'D BEEN A SIGN.
"A NEST. AN OWL NEST IN THE ATTIC. HE'D SHOOED THE BIRDS AWAY, BUT THEY'D COME BACK.
"IN AN OLDER VERSION OF THE RHYME, THERE'S A LINE ABOUT 'HEEDING THE SIGNS,' THE OMENS OF THE COURT.
"IN THE AFTERMATH OF THEIR DEATH, I SAW THE NEST AS A SIGN, A WARNING MY PARENTS HADN'T HEEDED.
"AND THEN AND THERE, I VOWED REVENGE.
"I WAS JUST A BOY, BUT I'D FIND THEM--THE COURT OF OWLS--AND I'D EXPOSE THEM. I'D CRUSH THEIR WORLD AS THEY HAD MINE."

"SO I BEGAN MY OWN INVESTIGATION INTO THE COURT. IN MANY WAYS, IT WAS MY FIRST CASE AS A *DETECTIVE*.
"AND I WAS *DETERMINED* TO SOLVE IT.
"IMMEDIATELY, CLUES BEGAN PRESENTING THEMSELVES.
"IN A MATTER OF DAYS, IT SEEMED EVERYWHERE I LOOKED THERE WAS SOME SIGN, SOME NEW PIECE OF EVIDENCE POINTING TO THE COURT'S EXISTENCE.
"SO I BEGAN DELVING *DEEPER*.
"IF THE COURT WAS MADE UP OF POWERFUL GOTHAM FAMILIES, THERE WAS NO BETTER PLACE TO START LOOKING THAN MY PARENTS' FRIENDS AND BUSINESS PARTNERS."
0 1 2 3 MI.
GOTHAM CITY

"DESPITE HIS WORK AS A DOCTOR, MY FATHER HAD BEEN DEEPLY INVOLVED IN THE CIVIC MECHANICS OF GOTHAM. NOT JUST CHARITIES, BUT EVERYTHING FROM MUSEUMS TO THE GOTHAM SHIPYARD.
"*ANYONE* COULD BE ONE OF THE COURT. NO ONE COULD BE RULED OUT.
"IN THE COURSE OF JUST A FEW WEEKS, I'D COMPILED NOTES ON SOME OF GOTHAM'S MOST PROMINENT FAMILIES. TO MY MIND--THE MIND OF A BOY DETECTIVE, ALL OF IT WAS EVIDENCE--EVIDENCE OF A FAR-REACHING CONSPIRACY AGAINST MY FAMILY.
"I'D EVEN LOCATED A BUILDING...AN OLD ABANDONED SOCIAL CLUB WITH A DOUBLE OWL ON THE CREST. A PLACE CALLED *HARBOR HOUSE*. IT WAS--"
"I KNOW IT."
"ALL OF THE FAMILIES I SUSPECTED HAD BELONGED TO THE CLUB AT ONE TIME OR ANOTHER.
"AND LOOKING AT THE SCHEMATICS OF THE BUILDING, I'D DISCOVERED A *ROOM* IN THE UPPER TOWER--WHAT LOOKED LIKE A WINDOWLESS MEETING PLACE, RIGHT ABOVE THE CREST OUTSIDE."

"I WAS SURE THIS WAS IT.
"I HAD FOUND THE COURT OF OWLS. THE MEN BEHIND MY PARENTS' DEATH.
"BUT WHAT I ACTUALLY FOUND THAT NIGHT...
"...UP THERE IN THAT SECRET ROOM, WAS SOMETHING MUCH MORE FRIGHTENING..."

"...DUST.
"NOTHING. NO ANSWERS. NO VILLAINS.
"JUST AN OLD, EMPTY ROOM THAT HADN'T BEEN USED IN YEARS.
"I WAS SO SHOCKED I DIDN'T SEE THE DOOR CLOSE BY MY FOOT.
"I WAS LOCKED UP THERE FOR OVER A *WEEK*.
"WHEN ALFRED FINALLY FOUND ME, I WAS ALREADY COMATOSE."

I SPENT THREE WEEKS IN THE HOSPITAL, RECOVERING.
WHEN I WOKE UP, THOUGH, I'D LEARNED A VALUABLE LESSON. A LESSON I BUILT MY SKILLS AS A *DETECTIVE* ON.
NEVER LET YOUR *EMOTIONS* GUIDE YOU ON A CASE.
I *NEEDED* THERE TO BE A COURT OF OWLS. SOME GREAT EVIL BEHIND MY PARENTS' MURDER. I LET THAT NEED GUIDE MY INVESTIGATION AND IT ALMOST KILLED ME.
YOU WERE JUST A *KID*, BRUCE.
I'VE LOOKED INTO THE COURT SINCE THEN AND ALWAYS COME UP EMPTY.
HOW *HARD* HAVE YOU LOOKED, THOUGH?
DEEPER THAN THE EVIDENCE WARRANTED.
BECAUSE THERE'S NEVER BEEN ANY.
LOOK, BRUCE. NO ONE KNOWS GOTHAM BETTER THAN YOU. IT'S YOUR CITY. IT'S *BATMAN'S CITY*...

"...BUT IT'S ALSO NEARLY FOUR HUNDRED YEARS OLD. WHICH MEANS, OVER THE YEARS, MAYBE IT BELONGED TO SOMETHING ELSE, TOO. SOMETHING BIG. SOMETHING DARK."
"I HAVE TO GO.
"I HAVE A LEAD TO FOLLOW UP ON."

My great, great grandfather Alan Wayne was behind the construction of some of Gotham's tallest towers.
His naked body was discovered here, beneath the city, in the sewers. The corpse had been down here so long that Alan had to be identified by the fillings in his **teeth.**
A nightmarish end for a man who spent so much time building Gotham up, to drown in its sewage.
The dirty blood of the city he helped build.
There are worse ways to go, though.
Like the way he **actually** went. Because examining his body myself, I discovered tiny punctures--not unlike stab wounds--in his bones. A lot of his bones, too.
Which is to say he was **stabbed** to death, most likely by throwing knives.
Almost **fifty** of them.

But I found something else on his bones.
A residue.
Dust from a metamorphic rock. Not unlike marble.
Strange, given that the sewer system is constructed almost entirely out of granite.
But that's Gotham. Never ceases to--

"THE COURT OF OWLS WATCHES, WATCHES ALL THE TIME.
"RULING GOTHAM FROM A SHADOWED PERCH, BEHIND GRANITE AND LIME.
"THEY SEE YOU AT YOUR HEARTH.
"AND THEY SEE YOU IN YOUR BED...
"... SPEAK NOT A WHISPERED WORD ABOUT THEM...
"... OR THEY'LL SEND THE TALON FOR YOUR HEAD!"

WELCOME, BATMAN, TO THE LABYRINTH!

Capullo
'11

Capullo '11

HE'LL BE DEAD SOON, YOU KNOW.
SIGGY. *THE BAT SIGNAL.*
YOU'VE BEEN RUNNING HIM HOT ALL WEEK. YOU'RE GOING TO BLOW HIS BULB.
LEAVE IT ON, HARVEY.

I HATE TO SAY IT, COMMISSIONER, BUT IT'S BEEN EIGHT DAYS.
THE BAT ISN'T COMING. LEAVING THE LIGHT ON FOR HIM--
IT'S NOT JUST FOR HIM, LIEUTENANT BULLOCK...
"...IT'S FOR THE SCUM WHO THINK GOTHAM'S A DAMN PLAYGROUND NOW.
"THE ONES WHO'RE HURTING.
NO TRANSMISSIO DETECTABLE.
"BECAUSE THEY KNOW HIM, THE MAN UNDERNEATH THAT MASK. THE MAN MISSING RIGHT NOW.

"IT'S FOR THE OTHER GUYS, TOO.
"THE ONES ON *OUR SIDE.*
"HELL, IT'S FOR THE *WHOLE CITY,* LIEUTENANT."
SO LIKE I SAID...

"...THE LIGHT STAYS ON."
They want me to come out of the dark... but I won't.
I won't.
I'll stay here.
Where it's safe.
Safe from them...

...from the Owls.
Here... again. Always here.
At the source.
Shouldn't drink...
...probably drugged. But I have to... so thirsty.
Like every part of me is crying out. Screaming.
Just a little. A sip.
No, no. Not too much!
Drink too much and...

Shhh. Stay still, Bruce.
They hear everything. They have special ears, asymmetrical, with one ear opening higher than the other, to locate prey.
And the way they watch. The eyes...
...hurry. No rope to climb. No belt...you have to go! Get out of here.
Away from the light.
Back to the dark...
...have to find the dark.

POP
How could I be here again?
Because it's a **story,** Bruce.
They're telling you a story. Room by room.
Over and over. Every part.
And this part of the story is all about the people they've **killed.** Here in this very maze.
**Hundreds** of people. Over hundreds of **years.** Hunted down. Something chasing them. A minotaur. Watching.
Once upon a time in Gotham... and **you're** the star now.
Smile.

NO... I WON'T LISTEN TO YOU!
I'M NOT LISTENING!
Keep your head straight, Bruce. Focus.
Get back in the dark.
The dark...
...where it's...
...safe?
I FOUND YOU! I'VE GOT YOU!

I'LL TEAR YOU LIMB...
...FROM LIMB...
YOU THINK YOU CAN FOOL ME?
YOU THINK SO?
You can't. Because I know all the tricks. Hell, I invented them.
And sooner or later...
...I will find you.
Wherever you are...
...you can't hide from me.
Hide in the dark. Because I live here...

...in the dark... in Gotham.
It's my city.
I know every alley.
Every rooftop.
So tell your story. With your pictures and your models and maps of Gotham through the years...
...try to tell me you've been here longer. That's what you're saying, right? That I don't matter?

That's why you didn't even bother to take off my mask?
And all these names, the names on the wall, they're people you used. Or members of your little flock. Or enemies you killed.
It's all the same to me.
All the same story. I've heard it all before.
GERALD
OBBLEPOT · BARNABUS
UEL GORDON · WILLIAM

Heard it all...
WELL, WELL.
Look at this. A new chapter. So what are you trying to tell me now?
With the talon on the wall. And these coffins.
These faces. Children.
Generations of children you turned into monsters, is that it? Young men and women you trained for years, so they could kill for you.
And one open? One missing?
What does it mean? That--
No!
Stop it, Bruce... I'm not listening.

Not listening.
Not listening.
Not listening!
Not listening!!
Not listening!!!
NOT--

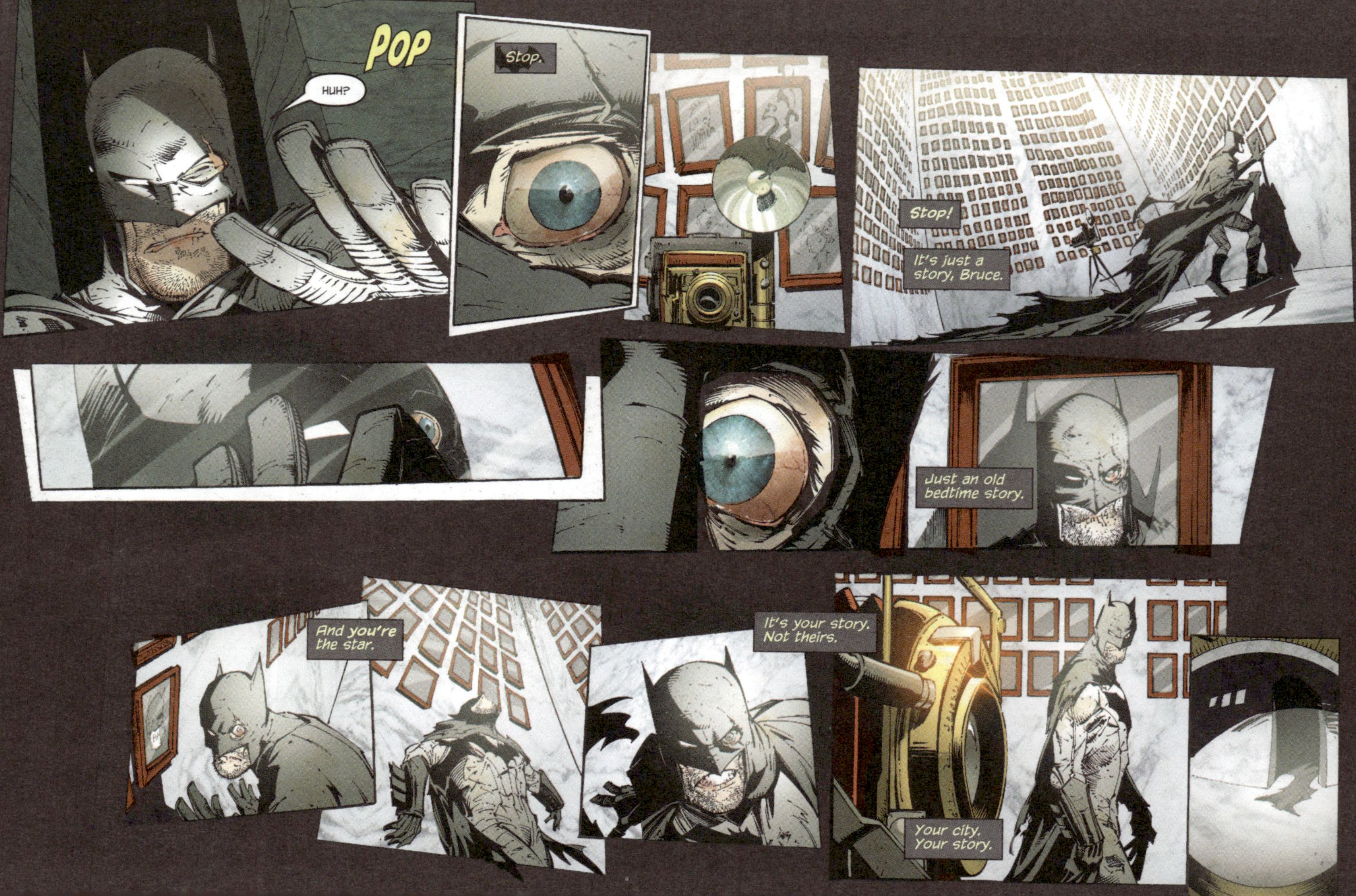
HUH?
POP
Stop.
Stop!
It's just a story, Bruce.
Just an old bedtime story.
And you're the star.
It's your story. Not theirs.
Your city. Your story.

Yours, Bruce.
Tell it.
You were born to...
...Thomas and Martha...
IT... IT CAN'T BE.
IT CAN'T!
MOTHER? FATHER?
BRUCE? MY GOD!
IS IT REALLY HIM, THOMAS? IS IT?
IT'S ME, YES!
BUT HOW... HOW?
WE'VE BEEN DOWN HERE SO LONG, BRUCE. *WAITING.*

IT *IS* YOU, ISN'T IT, BRUCE?
OF COURSE. DON'T YOU RECOGNIZE ME?
WE...WE CAN'T *SEE* ANYMORE, BRUCE. WE HAVEN'T BEEN ABLE TO FOR YEARS.
BUT... IT IS YOU, ISN'T IT?
IT'S ME. I FOUND YOU. I FOUND YOU.
OH, IF ONLY I COULD SEE YOU BRUCE.
WHAT I WOULDN'T GIVE TOOO *SEEEEEE...*
...EEEEEEEEEEE...
...EEEEEEEEEEEEEE
EEEEEEE
EEEEEEEEEEE
SCRATCH
SCRATCH
SCRATCH

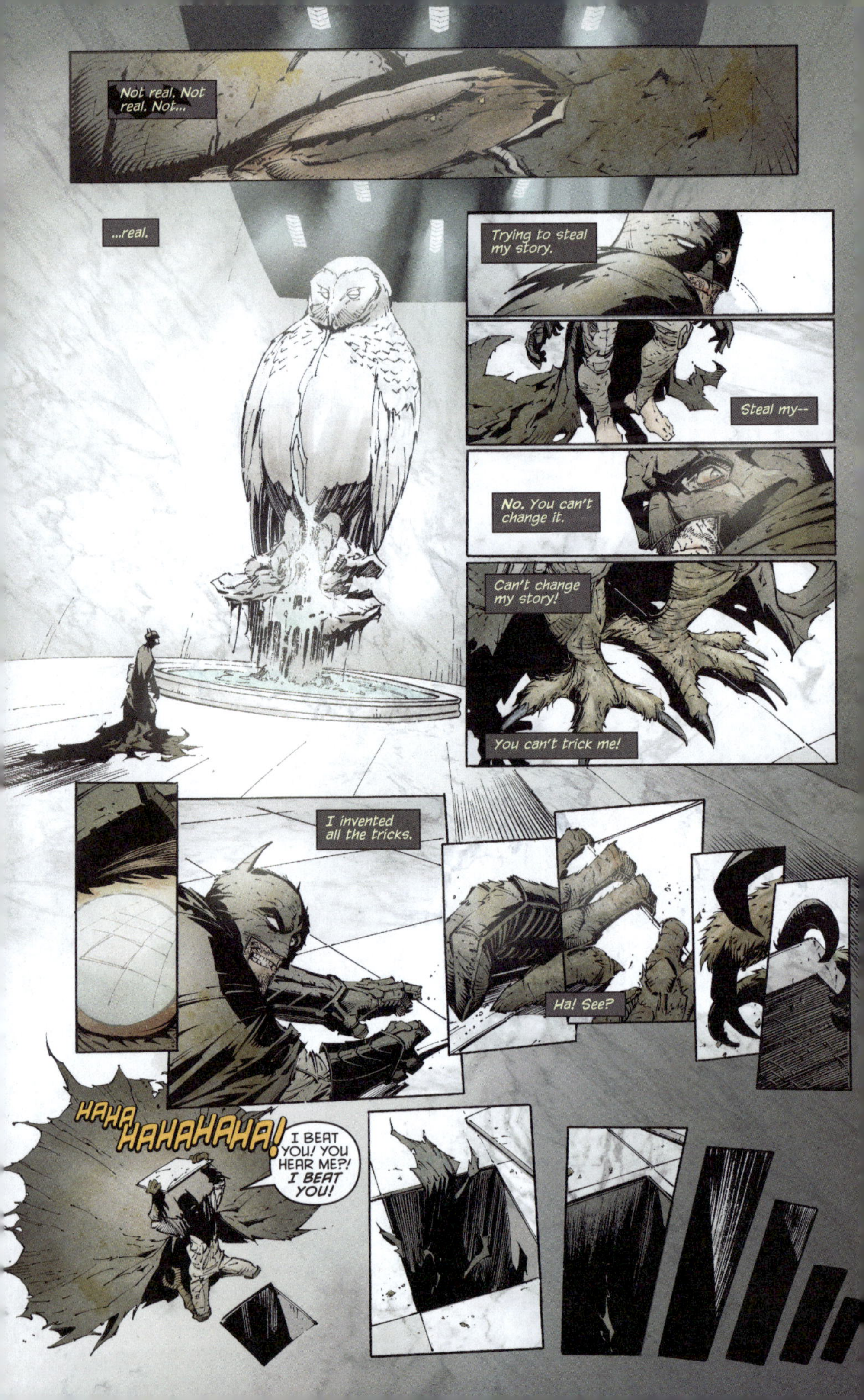
Not real. Not real. Not...
...real.
Trying to steal my story.
Steal my--
No. You can't change it.
Can't change my story!
You can't trick me!
I invented all the tricks.
Ha! See?
HAHA HAHAHAHAHA!
I BEAT YOU! YOU HEAR ME?! I BEAT YOU!

POP
No. It can't be.
No.
No.
NO!
NO. I'M NOT.
I'M NOT LISTENING!
I'M NOT LISTENING TO YOU!

WHAT SHOULD WE DO WITH IT?
GET A NEW ONE.
NOW.
I SAID NOW!
NOW... PLEASE.

Capullo '11

BATMAN, THE COURT OF OWLS HAS SENTENCED YOU TO DIE!

BUT YOU SHOULD DIE KNOWING THAT YOUR BODY WILL NOT BE RETURNED TO THE SURFACE!
BECAUSE THE COURT HAS DECIDED TO KEEP YOUR BONES DOWN HERE, TO BE DISPLAYED...
...IN THE LABYRINTH, FOREVER--A MONUMENT TO A VALIANT ENEMY.
ONLY THREE TIMES THROUGHOUT HISTORY HAS THE COURT HONORED SOMEONE IN THIS WAY.
DO YOU WISH TO SPEAK TO THIS HONOR, BEFORE YOUR DEATH?
HEH... YOU...
YES?
YOU MOVED THE CAMERA.

WHAK
NO FINAL ADDRESS, THEN. SO ALL THAT'S LEFT TO DO IS DECIDE THE MANNER OF YOUR DEATH.
MY COURT! MY COURT, HE IS PREPARED!
I PRESENT TO YOU THE BATMAN!
HOW DO YOU WISH HIM TO DIE?

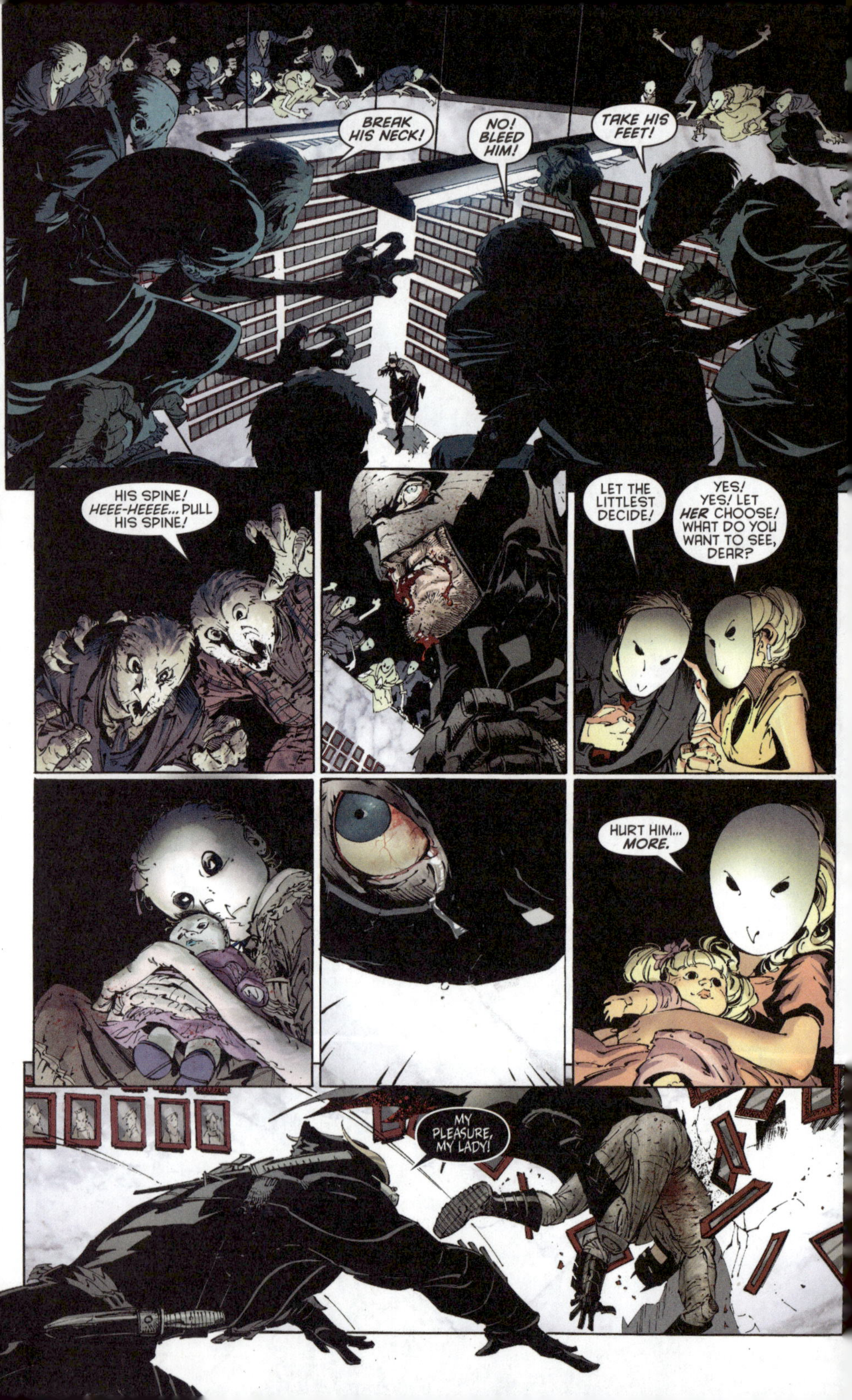
BREAK HIS NECK!
NO! BLEED HIM!
TAKE HIS FEET!
HIS SPINE! HEEE-HEEEE... PULL HIS SPINE!
LET THE LITTLEST DECIDE!
YES! YES! LET HER CHOOSE! WHAT DO YOU WANT TO SEE, DEAR?
HURT HIM... MORE.
MY PLEASURE, MY LADY!

HURT HIM LIKE THIS?
MORE!
MORE!
MOOORREEE!
LIKE THIS?!
MORE! MORE! MORE!
MORE! MORE! MORE!
AS YOU WISH, MY COURT!

IT IS DONE, MY COURT.
THE BATMAN IS FINISHED.
COME TAKE HIS BONES AS YOURS.
No...
...no strength left.
Blood f-filling the wrong...all the wrong places.
Whole body... every bone... saying let go.
Let go...and let them take you.

Let it end.
The pain.
The fight.
Become a ghost, a face behind the glass.
A face...
...his face...
Alan Wayne.
His face... so scared. Begging...
...calling out for someone.
Someone to help him...
...to help him stop... them.
Enough.

ENOUGH!

RUN!
HE'S STILL ALIVE!
WELL, WELL.
STILL SOME FIGHT IN YOU.
AND LOOK AT YOU.
HEH... BEATING YOUR WINGS.
GNASHING YOUR LITTLE FANGS.
DO YOU KNOW WHAT OWLS DO TO PREY THAT--
I KNOW...

...THAT I AM SICK...
...TO DEATH...
...OF OWLS!
WHAM

UNH!
ACK!

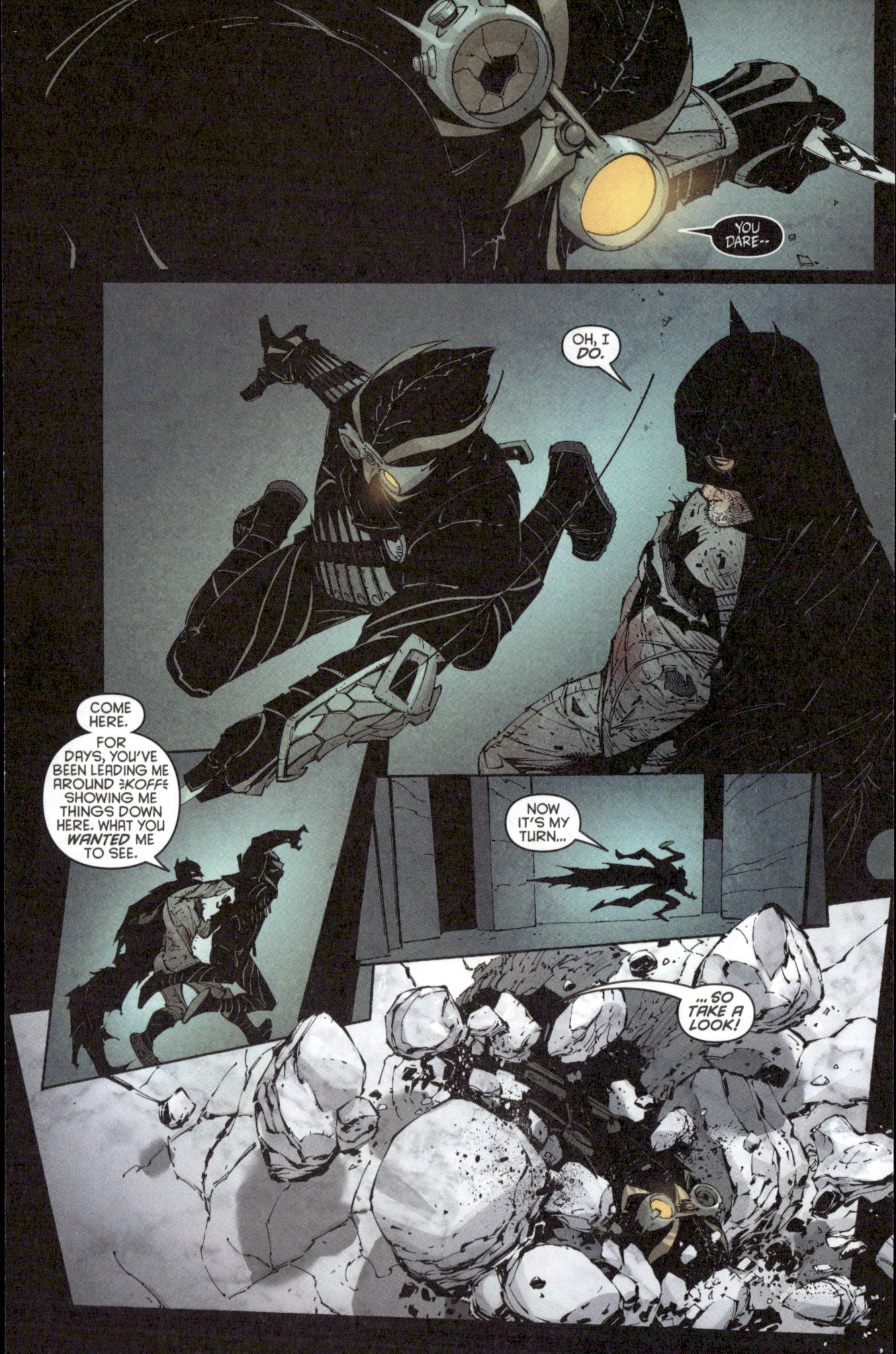
YOU DARE--
OH, I DO.
COME HERE.
FOR DAYS, YOU'VE BEEN LEADING ME AROUND *KOFF* SHOWING ME THINGS DOWN HERE. WHAT YOU WANTED ME TO SEE.
NOW IT'S MY TURN...
...SO TAKE A LOOK!

YOU SEE THIS? THE CITY AT YOUR FEET?
IT'S NOT THE REAL GOTHAM!
IT'S AN ARTS AND CRAFTS PROJECT!
UNH
UMMPH
BUT WAIT--
QUIET!
BUT THERE'S MORE...
...BECAUSE YOU, TALON--
I SAID QUIET!
I SEE WHAT YOU ARE, TOO. YOU'RE NOTHING...
SHUT UP!

...BUT A HIRED THUG!
YOU'RE A PAWN.
YOU'RE NOT SPECIAL!
NO MATTER WHAT THEY'VE TOLD YOU!
NO MATTER WHAT YOU TELL YOURSELF!
AND NOW...
...WHAT YOU REALLY ARE...
...IS FINISHED.

DO YOU ≷KOFF KOFF≶ DO YOU HEAR ME, COURT OF OWLS?
WHOEVER YOU ARE.
THAT... THAT GOES FOR ALL OF YOU.
YOU HEAR ME?!
YOU CAN'T HIDE FROM ME. I KNOW THIS CITY, DOWN TO ITS FOUNDATION.
FOR EXAMPLE, I KNOW THAT THIS PLACE--THE TASTE OF THE WATER IN THE FOUNTAIN, THE MINERALS...
...WE'RE NEAR THE RIVER. AND I KNOW THE BASE OF YOUR BIG UGLY FOUNTAIN...IT'S ≷KOFF≶ WHITE MARBLE. NOT CONSTRUCTION MARBLE LIKE THE REST OF THIS PLACE.
WHICH MAKES IT SOFTER, MORE VULNERABLE TO, SAY... EXPLOSIONS.
AND YOU KNOW WHAT EXPLODES? POTASSIUM CHLORATE. WHEN IT IGNITES.
WHICH IS WHY I SLIPPED OUT THE SUPPLY OF FILAMENT PLATES FROM YOUR CAMERA BEFORE.

BOOM
KOFF KOFF...I'LL BE BACK FOR YOU. ALL OF YOU!
UNH...
KOFF...
Out...
...must...get out now.

Get out and go home...
...home to the cave and never...
...never come back here.
GASP!

No...
...can't get away.
Can't break through the glass.
They won't ever let me go.
The Court...
...I'm already dead, aren't I?
Bones in the dark.
Nothing but a dead face...
...a face.

WELL, *THAT* WAS THRILLING!
WHAT A WONDERFUL GLADIATOR, THE BATMAN.
YES. YES, HE IS.
WHAT SHOULD WE DO WITH *THIS* ONE?
YES, WHAT?
WE SHOULD *DISPOSE* OF HIM.
HERE.
WAIT! BUT THE INVESTMENT IN HIM...AND HE'LL HEAL IF YOU GIVE HIM--
NOT TRULY, HE WON'T. NOT IN THE IMPORTANT WAY. NOT FROM *THAT* BEATING.

OH, DON'T WORRY, MY DEAR. WE HAVE SO MANY MORE OF THEM!
NOW, ALL WE HAVE TO DO IS WAKE THEM UP.
ALL OF THEM!

"SOME ANCIENTS BELIEVED THAT THE MOMENT OF DEATH BROUGHT WITH IT *VISIONS*.
"NOT JUST VISIONS OF ONE'S PAST, OR OF THINGS KNOWN TO THE DYING...
"...BUT VISIONS OF ONE'S SELF AS ONE TRULY EXISTED IN LIFE..."
YES...
...YES. FATHER, I SHALL BECOME A *BAT*.

"THEY BELIEVED, THE ANCIENTS, THAT THESE FINAL VISIONS OFTEN WENT BEYOND WHAT WAS KNOWN TO THE DYING MAN IN LIFE...
"...THAT THEY CONSTITUTED SECRET TRUTHS ABOUT HIS LIFE, REVEALED.
"SOME TRUTHS WERE COMFORTING...SOME WERE HEART-SHATTERING.
"EITHER WAY, THESE VISIONS WERE MEANT TO OFFER A SENSE OF CLOSURE SO THAT HE MAY LEAVE THE WORLD IN PEACE, KNOWING ALL THERE WAS TO KNOW ABOUT HIMSELF.
"A VISION OF HIMSELF AS HE TRULY WAS. REFLECTED IN THE BURNING EYES OF HIS GOD."
"COME BACK!"

I KNOW YOU CAN HEAR ME! COME ON!
THAT'S IT, THAT'S IT... DAMN IT!
COME ON, WORK, WORK. WORK!
AAAARGHHH!
ZZZZZTT
WAIT! WHO ARE YOU?!
IT'S JUST...

...ME.
YOU.
I'M SORRY...
...THE JUMPERS WERE ALL I HAD. YOU FLAT-LINED AND THIS IS MY BOSS' VAN AND--
I TOLD YOU ONCE ALREADY...
...LEAVE ME ALONE.
I *MEANT* IT.
NICE ONE, HARPER. EPIC BAT-FAIL.
"BUT LEGEND HAS IT, IF A DYING MAN RESISTS THE VISIONS, RESISTS THE PULL TOWARD TRUTH AND JOURNEYS BACK TO THE LAND OF THE LIVING...
"...HE MAY FIND HIMSELF *GREATLY CHANGED* UPON RETURN."

"AND YOU--YOU WHO STAND BEFORE US NOW--WILL CERTAINLY FIND YOURSELF CHANGED...
"...WHEN YOU OPEN YOUR EYES.
"WHICH YOU WILL DO NOW..."
...YES, OPEN THOSE EYES FOR US. OPEN YOUR EYES FOR YOUR COURT!
YOU HAVE TRAVELED SO FAR, FROM THE BANKS OF THE RIVER LETHE, THE RIVER OF MINDLESSNESS, WHERE THE SHADES WALK, BACK TO THIS WORLD, TO YOUR CITY.
GOTHAM.
YES, LOOK... LOOK AT YOUR BODY. IT HAS BEEN RESTORED, AND MADE STRONGER THAN BEFORE. MUCH STRONGER.
YOU DRANK FROM THE CUP OF IMMORTALITY, AND YOU CANNOT BE KILLED. YOUR WOUNDS IN BATTLE WILL HEAL.
YOU ARE FASTER, STRONGER THAN EVER.
AND WE ARE STRONGER, TOO. YOUR COURT. WE HAVE BEEN GATHERING OUR RESOURCES, OUR POWER, AND WAITING AS THE GREAT OWL WAITS-- IN PLAIN SIGHT.
UNTIL NOW...
...FOR NOW IT IS TIME FOR US TO STRIKE...TO RECLAIM THIS CITY...

"...AND RIP OUT THE HEART OF OUR ENEMY."
HALT!
NO TRESPASSING
IDENTIFY YOURSELF!
IT'S... ME.

MASTER BRUCE! MY GOD...
...WHEN I SAW THE HOLE IN THE ICE, I CONCLUDED THAT YOU'D CLIMBED OUT OF THE HARBOR YOURSELF.
BUT WHEN YOU NEVER APPEARED, I FEARED ONE OF YOUR ENEMIES HAD REMOVED YOU AND--
IT WAS... SOMEONE ELSE.
PASSWORD: "FAIRBANKS"
NO...

NO!
HE'S DEAD, SIR.
WE DISCOVERED HIS BODY IN THE FROZEN WATER, NEAR THE SPOT WE DETECTED THE SHORT BEACON FROM YOUR SUIT.
I MOVED HIS BODY HERE TO THE BATCAVE FOR EXAMINATION.
LET'S GET YOU TO THE MEDICAL STATION.
NO.
BUT, SIR--
GET HIM ON THE TABLE.
"LOOK UPON OUR ENEMY. THE BAT."

LOOK UPON HIS IMAGE.
LIKE YOU, HE HAS JUST NOW JOURNEYED UP FROM THE *UNDERWORLD.*
BUT WHILE YOU HAVE RETURNED STRONGER, MORE POWERFUL, HE HAS RETURNED *BROKEN* AND *WEAK.*
WE HAVE MOVED YOUR ARMOR HERE, YOUR ARMS.
WE ASK YOU NOW TO LET US ARM YOU, ARM YOU FOR *BATTLE.*
FOR TONIGHT, WE WILL *STRIKE DOWN* OUR ENEMY.
NOT JUST STRIKE HIM DOWN, BUT TEAR HIM APART.
*LIMB FROM LIMB.*
AND EAT HIS *BONES.*

BRUCE?
I ASKED ALFRED--
TO TELL ME YOU NEEDED PRIVACY, I KNOW, BUT I WANTED TO COME DOWN AND SEE YOU.
GEEZ, BRUCE. WHAT DID THEY...DO TO YOU?

THE MAN ON THE TABLE IS THE TALON.
AN ASSASSIN FOR THE COURT OF OWLS.
IS HE... DEAD?
YES...
...AND NO.
THERE'S A COMPOUND I'VE ISOLATED IN HIS CELLS. SOMETHING THE COURT MUST HAVE MANAGED TO SYNTHESIZE. IT'S CAPABLE OF REANIMATING DEAD TISSUE.
BRINGING BODIES BACK FROM THE DEAD?
ONLY BODIES SPECIALLY PREPARED.
PREPARED HOW?
THE COURT HAS AN AFFINITY FOR CLASSICAL ANTIQUITY. IN ANCIENT GREECE, THERE WAS A TRADITION OF PLACING COINS BENEATH THE CORPSE'S TONGUE BEFORE BURIAL. SUPPOSEDLY TO PAY FOR PASSAGE INTO HADES.
THE RICH SOMETIMES HAD THEIR COINS MADE FROM A METAL CALLED ELECTRUM. A HIGHLY CONDUCTIVE ALLOY OF SILVER AND COPPER.
IN THIS MAN'S BODY, I FOUND A SIGNIFICANT AMOUNT OF ELECTRUM.
NOT JUST IN HIS BLOOD, BUT IN HIS CELLS. THE ALLOY SEEPED DOWN OVER YEARS AND YEARS, FROM A DEPOSIT EMBEDDED IN HIS TOOTH. IN THE SHAPE OF A TINY OWL.
LIKE THE JOHN DOE HE KILLED--HE CARRIED HIS FERRYMAN'S COIN WITH HIM ALL THE TIME, FOR YEARS.
BY THE TIME HE WAS RETIRED HE WAS A WALKING CONDUCTOR, WAITING FOR A SPARK. AND FROM A CHEMIST'S STANDPOINT, THAT'S ALL THIS COMPOUND IS.
A SPARK TO LIGHT UP THE WIRE.

SO THEY USED THE COMPOUND TO BRING HIM BACK FROM THE DEAD TO *KILL* FOR THEM.
AND HIS FIRST TARGET WAS HIS OLD TRAINER, THE JOHN DOE. AFTER ALL, WHO NEEDS THE COACH ANYMORE WHEN YOU CAN REANIMATE YOUR STAR ATHLETE?
AND HIS HEALING FACTOR?
ONCE THE COMPOUND IS BONDED WITH THE CELLS, THEY'RE CAPABLE OF REACTIVATING AND HEALING OVER AND OVER.
WHICH IS WHY HE WAS ABLE TO WALK AWAY FROM THE FALL OFF WAYNE TOWER.
AND WHY HE'S TECHNICALLY *STILL ALIVE* RIGHT NOW. SO HOW DO YOU TAKE HIM DOWN?
THE *COLD.* THE COMPOUND TURNS THE BODY INTO A KIND OF HEAT-POWERED FACTORY FOR CELL REGROWTH.
THE WAY TO SHUT IT DOWN IS TO LOWER THE HOST'S CORE BODY TEMPERATURE. PUT HIM BACK ON ICE. I'M RUNNING FREEZING SOLUTION INTO HIM NOW.
DO YOU HAVE A NAME FOR HIM YET?
YES. HIS NAME IS COBB. *WILLIAM COBB.*
AND HE'S YOUR *GREAT-GRANDFATHER.*

MY... MY WHAT?
I TOOK A TISSUE SAMPLE, DICK.
AND WHAT, YOU WEREN'T GOING TO TELL ME?
THAT'S WHY YOU WANTED PRIVACY?
THAT'S ONE PART OF IT, YES.
AND YOU'RE NOT GOING TO TELL ME THE OTHER PART.
HEH. OF COURSE YOU'RE NOT.

YOU KNOW, BRUCE, I GET THAT YOU THINK YOU'RE PROTECTING ME BY KEEPING YOUR SECRETS.
OR RATHER, I GET THAT YOU WANT TO THINK THAT'S WHY YOU KEEP SECRETS LIKE THIS.
BUT SINCE WE'RE BEING SO HONEST AND UP FRONT--RIGHT? LET'S JUST ADMIT THAT BOTH OF US KNOW THE PERSON YOU'RE REALLY PROTECTING IS YOURSELF.
FROM NEEDING TO HAVE A DAMN HUMAN EMOTION!
BUT YOU HAVE NO IDEA WHAT I'VE BEEN THROUGH THESE LAST FEW WEEKS! NO IDEA! THE THINGS I'VE HAD TO DEAL WITH!
AND I'LL TELL YOU WHAT, BRUCE, IF YOU THINK LEARNING MY ANCESTOR, SOME GUY I NEVER EVEN KNEW, WAS A CRIMINAL--
--IF YOU THINK THAT'S GOING TO FAZE ME, THEN FRANKLY, YOU DON'T KNOW ME AT--

KRACK

I...I WAS SUPPOSED TO BE A... TALON?
YOU WERE SUPPOSED TO BE ONE, TOO, DICK.
IN PRE-MODERN TIMES, POTENTIAL GLADIATORS WERE SOMETIMES ESCORTED TO THE COLISEUMS BY PARADES OF PERFORMERS. JESTERS AND ACROBATS. AN ANCIENT VERSION OF THE--
CIRCUS...
...OF COURSE...
...BUT HOW DID YOU KNOW?
HE CAME TO SEE YOU FIRST. THE TRAINER OF THE COURT'S LAST TALONS. OUR JOHN DOE. THE IDENTITY OF THIS TALON HERE SIMPLY CONFIRMED IT.
EVERY DECADE, HALY'S CIRCUS PRESENTED A CROP OF CHILD ATHLETES TO THE COURT, AND THE MEMBERS CHOSE ONE IN SECRET TO BE TRAINED AS THAT ERA'S TALON.
YOU WERE MEANT TO BE THE MOST RECENT ONE. BUT WHEN YOUR PARENTS DIED...
AND YOU TOOK ME IN...

YOU KNOW, SOME NIGHTS, DICK, ON PATROL, I'VE FELT THE CITY LOOKING AT ME. I ALWAYS THOUGHT IT WAS WATCHING OVER ME, THOUGH, LIKE A PARTNER, OR EVEN FAMILY...
...YOU ASKED ME BEFORE, WHAT THE COURT DID TO ME.
WHAT THEY DID WAS SHOW ME THE TRUTH. THAT THE GOTHAM CITY I THOUGHT I KNEW, MY CITY... DOESN'T EXIST.
THEY SHOWED ME THAT THE REAL GOTHAM, THE GOTHAM OUT THERE, IS A CITY OF BIRDS. A CITY OF OWLS.
IT'S A STRANGER AND AN ENEMY... IT ALWAYS HAS BEEN.
AND I'LL TELL YOU, DICK, IF SOMEONE COULD'VE PROTECTED ME FROM THAT TRUTH, I'D HAVE BEEN GRATEFUL.
WELL, HERE'S SOME TRUTH FOR YOU.
YOU MIGHT BE SEEING SIDES ALREADY, ALL OF US BIRDS ON ONE AND YOU, THE BAT, ON THE OTHER. HELL, YOU'RE PROBABLY THROWING UP WALLS RIGHT AND LEFT.
BUT THE FACT IS, I DON'T CARE WHO MY ANCESTOR WAS. OR WHAT THE COURT OF OWLS WANTED ME TO BE. I DON'T. WE ARE WHO WE CHOOSE TO BE, BRUCE. NOT THE ROLE THE PAST SAYS WE SHOULD PLAY.
THE COURT OF OWLS IS JUST ANOTHER BAD GUY, BRUCE. THEY'RE A LITTLE GRAYER AROUND THE TEMPLES IS ALL.
YES, YOU MADE A MISTAKE AND UNDERESTIMATED THEM...

"...BUT THEY'RE NOT GOTHAM CITY, BRUCE.
"AND NEITHER ARE *YOU*."
YES, THIS WAY!
COME SEE!
FOR TONIGHT WE WILL NOT ONLY *KILL OUR ENEMY*, BUT WE WILL *TAKE BACK OUR CITY!*
*WE WILL TAKE BACK OUR KINGDOM!*

NOW GO! GO AND TAKE GOTHAM CITY!

Capullo
11
+fco

# CHAPTER EIGHT • ATTACK ON WAYNE MANOR

NIGHT OF THE OWLS, 7:01 PM...
I've always believed the best way to know the city is to stay close to the ground.
To feel the cracks in the sidewalk under your shoes.
The strange bright silence of the park under snow.
The hissing rain of sparks that comes down when the elevated train passes overhead on Third Avenue.
The late night ticking of traffic lights.
It's only been in the last few weeks that I've come to understand how **wrong** I've been.
Because I know now that you can spend your whole life learning Gotham from deep inside...

...and still know nothing about it at all.

SHUT IT OFF, ALFRED. IT'S HURTING MY EYES.
IF YOU WISH, SIR. BUT THEY SAY LOW-LEVEL LASER ILLUMINATION CAN BE THERAPEUTIC FOR EYE INJURIES.
YOU WANT A METAPHOR, OLD FRIEND, HERE'S ONE...

...I'M A MAN STANDING OVER A TOY CITY HE MADE HIMSELF WHILE THE REAL ONE, THE ONE THAT MATTERS, OPERATES BEHIND HIS BACK.
I WASN'T TRADING IN WORDPLAY, SIR. YOU'VE BEEN SITTING IN THE DARK FOR HOURS.
AND YOU HAVE INFLAMMATION IN MOST OF THE TISSUE AROUND YOUR EYES AND A CONJUNCTIVAL HEMORRHAGE IN--
I'VE BEEN A FOOL, ALFRED.
AN ARROGANT FOOL.
PERHAPS. BUT THEN YOU COME FROM A LONG LINE OF SUCH MEN, SIR. AND THAT CITY ACROSS THE BAY IS A BETTER PLACE FOR ALL OF THEIR ARROGANT FOOLISHNESS.

AND IF YOU--
THUMP
SIR--
I HEARD IT. SOMEONE'S TRYING TO GET IN.
GET TO THE CAVE. I'LL TAKE CARE OF THE INTRUDER.
BUT SIR, I CAN--
I HAVE THE EARPIECE AND LENS.
HELP ME FROM DOWN THERE.
"GO!"

SIR, I'M IN POSITION.
I'M PICKING UP INTRUDER SIGNALS ALL AROUND THE MANOR, BUT THEY'RE NOT MAKING SENSE...
...THE PULSES ARE...
...OH, NO...
MASTER BRUCE, YOU MUST GET DOWN HERE!
BRUCE WAYNE...
...THE COURT OF OWLS...
...HAS SENTENCED YOU TO--

MASTER BRUCE!
CRASH
CRACK
YEAH, I GOT IT THE FIRST TIME!

HA, HA! SEEMS YOU HAVE SOME MOVES, MR. WAYNE!
WELL SO DO I!
MAYBE SO. BUT YOURS...
...WENT OUT OF STYLE TWO HUNDRED YEARS AGO!
ALFRED.
ALFRED, I NEED POSITIONS.
ALFRED!

I'M... I'M TRYING, SIR!
BUT THEY'RE ALL AROUND YOU!
YES, I CAN SEE THAT. BUT OTHERS--
THAT'S WHAT I MEAN, SIR! THERE ARE SO MANY OTHERS!
AND THEY'RE GETTING INTO THE HOUSE FROM ALL SIDES!
SIR, YOU NEED HELP! I CAN--
HOO HOO.
ALFRED? ALFRED, ARE YOU THERE?

ALFRED?
DAMN.
WHAK
UNH!

GO AHEAD, BRUCE! TRY TO RUN AWAY!
WE'LL FOLLOW YOU WHEREVER YOU GO!
YOU WON'T.
ARGH!
BROTHERS... I AM PINNED.
NOWHERE LEFT TO GO, BRUCE.

NOWHERE TO RUN...YOU'RE GOING DOWN. NOW.
DEEEET
GOOD CHOICE OF WORDS.
WHAT--
GET HIM! HE'S ESCAPING!
IT'S LOCKED!
WE'LL GET YOU, BRUCE WAYNE!
WE'RE COMING FOR YOU!

Stupid, Bruce. Stupid.
You should have seen this coming.
You should have been watching for it.
Not lost in your own head.
ALFRED!
ALFRED, ARE YOU ALL RI--
WELL, WELL.
SEEMS YOU HAVE A SECRET, BRUCE. DON'T YOU?

CREAK...
HUH?
NO!
CLANG
YOUR LUCKY PENNY, SIR.
HEH. ARE YOU ALL RIGHT?
QUITE, SIR.
GOOD. NOW LET'S GET SOME ANSWERS.

HOW MANY? I SAID HOW MANY ARE COMING FOR US?!
ENOUGH. AND NOT JUST FOR YOU...
...BUT DON'T WORRY, YOU'LL FIND OUT SOON.
OR SOONER.
AAAAARRGH! YOU'RE... YOU'RE *KOFF!* BREAKING MY ARM!
CRACK
CORRECT.
NOW LOOK WHAT WE HAVE HERE!
OH, BRUCE!

"WE'RE COMING FOR YOU.
"YOU CAN'T STOP THE COURT.
"YOU CAN'T HOLD US BACK.
"THERE'S NOWHERE TO RUN ANYMORE.
"WE'RE IN THE HEART OF YOUR HOUSE, BRUCE! THE HOUSE OF WAYNE! AND OF BATMAN!"
THE ARMORY, ALFRED! GET INSIDE!
SIR--
QUICKLY!
THAT'S OKAY, BRUCE. WE'LL FIND A WAY IN.
WE ALWAYS DO.

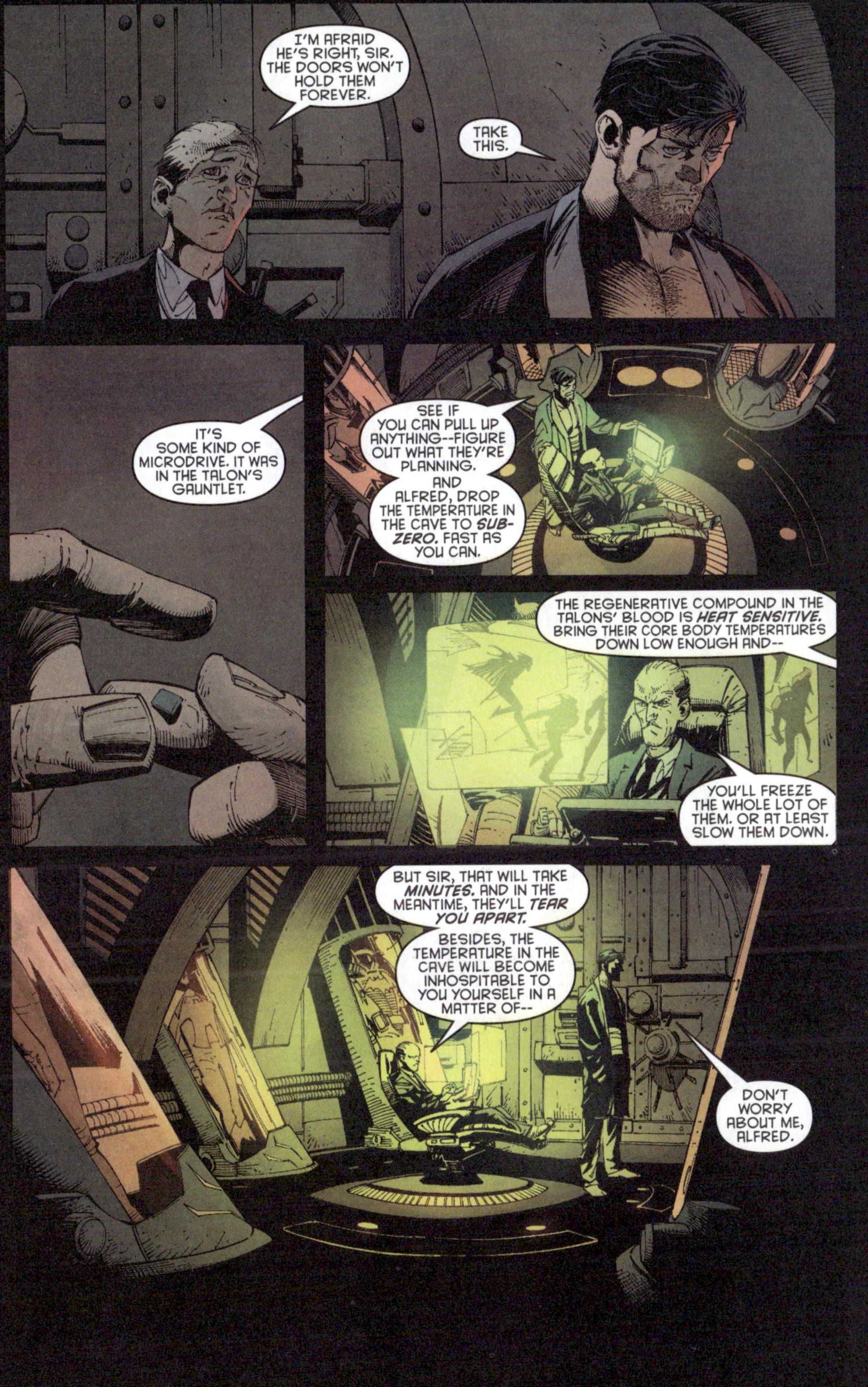
I'M AFRAID HE'S RIGHT, SIR. THE DOORS WON'T HOLD THEM FOREVER.
TAKE THIS.
IT'S SOME KIND OF MICRODRIVE. IT WAS IN THE TALON'S GAUNTLET.
SEE IF YOU CAN PULL UP ANYTHING--FIGURE OUT WHAT THEY'RE PLANNING.
AND ALFRED, DROP THE TEMPERATURE IN THE CAVE TO *SUB-ZERO.* FAST AS YOU CAN.
THE REGENERATIVE COMPOUND IN THE TALONS' BLOOD IS *HEAT SENSITIVE.* BRING THEIR CORE BODY TEMPERATURES DOWN LOW ENOUGH AND--
YOU'LL FREEZE THE WHOLE LOT OF THEM. OR AT LEAST SLOW THEM DOWN.
BUT SIR, THAT WILL TAKE *MINUTES.* AND IN THE MEANTIME, THEY'LL *TEAR YOU APART.*
BESIDES, THE TEMPERATURE IN THE CAVE WILL BECOME INHOSPITABLE TO YOU YOURSELF IN A MATTER OF--
DON'T WORRY ABOUT ME, ALFRED.

"I'M SURE I'VE GOT SOMETHING WARM IN HERE."
YOU CAN'T HIDE FOREVER, BRUCE!
THAT'S WHAT WAYNES ALWAYS TRY TO DO, BUT IT'S NO USE.
SO GO ON, LITTLE BRUCE, AND...
...OPEN UP?

GET THE HELL OUT OF MY HOUSE.

# CHAPTER NINE • NIGHT OF THE OWLS

The first members of my family to live in the manor were Solomon and Joshua Wayne--brothers. They bought the house in 1855.
But they didn't move in until two years later.
The reason was **bats.**
A massive infestation of bats in the cave system beneath the land.
They brought in a chiroptologist from Gotham University, and according to him, to get rid of the bats, they'd have to introduce a **predator** into the cave.
So the Wayne brothers did.
They carted in all sorts of birds, from Peregrine Falcons to kestrels, and unleashed them in differrent sections of the cave.
The most effective killers of bats, though, were the **tiger owls.**
My ancestors let owls loose in the cave...

NIGHT OF THE OWLS, 7:51 PM...
...and within a year, all the bats were gone.
ALFRED. HOW ARE WE DOING ON TEMPERATURE?

I'M DROPPING IT AS FAST AS POSSIBLE, SIR.

IT NEEDS TO BE FASTER.
IT SHOULD DIP BELOW ZERO IN NO MORE THAN A MINUTE. DROP TO NEGATIVE TWENTY, MAYBE EVEN THIRTY, IN UNDER FIVE MINUTES.
BY THEN THE RESTORATIVE COMPOUND IN THE TALONS' CELLS SHOULD BEGIN TO FREEZE. BUT SIR, I IMPLORE YOU, COME BACK INSIDE THE ARMORY!
THEY'RE STRONG, ALFRED. THE DOORS WON'T KEEP THEM OUT LONG ENOUGH.
THE DOORS MAY!
NO.
MASTER BRUCE, THE TALONS' STRENGTH, THEIR HEALING CAPABILITIES, PLEASE, FOR YOU IT MEANS CERTAIN--
WHAT IT MEANS, ALFRED...
...IS THAT I CAN PLAY ROUGH FOR ONCE.

My suit is built for war.
It's made of meta-aramid fibers of my own design, tougher than Kevlar.
Made to withstand burning heat and freezing cold--temperatures as low as the Arctic winter.
It uses a semi-solid flow micro battery. It has enough oxygen for weeks.
Meaning, it's built for battle in the most alien territories on Earth.
And I'm wearing it here. In my own home.
COME ON!
I SAID COME ON, YOU UNDEAD SONS OF--

Alfred is right...
CLANG
...they'll get through the suit, the Talons.
Because in a way, they already have.
MASTER BRUCE!
WUMP
HE'S DOWN, BROTHERS!
GET HIM!

THIS IS IT, BRUCE WAYNE.
NOTHING LEFT TO KEEP US OUT. NO MORE BARRIERS.
THE COURT ALWAYS FINDS A WAY INTO YOUR HOME!
YOU WAYNES ALWAYS TRY, THOUGH, DON'T YOU?
WELL, GO AHEAD! TRY WHATEVER YOU LIKE!
MORE GATES. MORE ALARMS.
(HEH) MAYBE TRY A GUARD DOG.
ACTUALLY, *KOFF* I ALREADY HAVE ONE.

"Activate Fido."
WHUMP
GOOD BOY.

YOU THINK THAT WILL STOP US?
YOUR LITTLE PARLOR TR-- UNH!
MASTER BRUCE, YOUR VITAL SIGNS... YOU'RE GOING TO BLACK OUT!
I'VE GOT HIM! SAY GOODBYE, WAYNE!
MASTER BRUCE!
I'M COMING OUT TO HELP YOU!

ARMORY DOORS--
NO! OVERRIDE ARMORY DOORS! LOCK DOWN!
NO! MASTER BRUCE!
MASTER BRUCE, YOU'RE CRASHING!
My ancestors... they used owls to kill the bats.
Owls everywhere.
But I forgot... the thing I forgot is...
...as soon as the owls left...

...the bats...
...came back.

Yes...
...I remember now.
The bats had simply hidden deeper in the caves.
In the darkest parts, the parts the owls couldn't tolerate.
And when the bats came back...
...it was with a vengeance.

SIR, IT'S NEGATIVE TWENTY AND DROPPING.
THE TALONS SHOULD BE FEELING THE EFFECTS OF THE COLD BY NOW. BUT PLEASE, SIR, EXPOSED TO SUCH COLD, YOUR VITAL SIGNS--
THE COLD BROUGHT THE BATS OUT OF THE DARK, ALFRED.
I FEEL... FINE.
SIR, ONE OF THEM IS HEADED FOR THE BRIDGE, TRYING TO MAKE AN ESCAPE.
OH, I SEE HIM.

AAAACH!
SIR...!
HE'S GOT A HEALING FACTOR.
LET HIM HEAL.
USE THE COOLANT I PREPARED FOR COBB TO *FREEZE* THE TALONS.
YES, SIR, BUT YOU MUST STAY HERE AND--
THERE'S AN OWL SYMBOL IN THE SKY OVER GOTHAM, ALFRED. I'M GOING OUT.

NIGHT OF THE OWLS, 8:36 PM...
THE LIST OF PEOPLE THE COURT OF OWLS IS TARGETING...
AND THE ONES IN RED?
I'M AFRAID FOR THEM IT'S ALREADY TOO LATE. THE GREEN NAMES. THEY'RE THE ONLY TARGETS STILL UNACCOUNTED FOR.
THERE ARE BARELY ANY GREEN, ALFRED. JUST JEREMIAH ARKHAM AND LINCOLN MARCH.
NIGHT OF THE OWLS, 11:02 PM...
"AND THEN I'LL GO AFTER MARCH."

I'M SENDING IT TO THE MAIN CONSOLE. THE NAMES IN BLUE, THEY'RE THE ONES THE ALLIES HAVE ALREADY GONE TO PROTECT.
"I'M AFRAID THIS NIGHT LARGELY BELONGS TO THE OWLS, SIR."
"THE NIGHT'S NOT OVER YET.
"I'M GOING TO ARKHAM ASYLUM FIRST."
LINCOLN MARCH!
I'M HERE TO HELP! MARCH?!

MR. MARCH, I--
YOU...
...BRUCE WAYNE...
MARCH
BLAM

...
THUMP
MARCH
*KOFF* FOR BRUCE WAYNE...
MARCH
...I HAVE A MESSAGE FOR BRUCE WAYNE.

2012
LINCOLN
MARCH
DON'T TALK, MR. MARCH. AN AMBULANCE WILL BE HERE ANY MOMENT.
NO... PLEASE. HERE...
...HERE. TAKE THIS.
THERE ARE THREE NAMES *KOFF*. I TRIED TO FOLLOW THE DONATIONS TO FIGURE IT OUT... IT'S AS CLOSE AS I GOT.
COULD BE ALL THREE OF THEM ARE IN THE COURT. COULD BE *KOFF* NONE.
MR. MARCH, THE MORE YOU TALK--
I'M DEAD. HE KILLED ME. I GOT HIM BACK, THOUGH. ARMOR PIERCING, HEH. FRIEND ON THE FORCE...
BUT, BRUCE...
...BRUCE... YOU KNOW HIM. PLEASE, TELL HIM TO FIGHT THEM. THIS CITY, IT'S WORTH IT. IT CAN BE A GOOD PLACE.
REMIND HIM THAT... A BETTER GOTHAM IS JUST... *KOFF*... IS ONE DREAM...

MASTER BRUCE. THE TALONS HAVE BEEN CONTAINED. I HAVE NEWS ON THE OTHER ASSASSINATION ATTEMPTS, AS WELL.
I KNOW WHERE THEY LIVE, ALFRED.
BUT, SIR--
THEY CAME TO MY HOUSE...
G·O·T·H·A·M
...NOW I'M GOING TO BURN *THEIRS* TO THE GROUND.
G·O·T·H·A·M

Capullo 12
+fco

# CHAPTER TEN • ASSAULT ON THE COURT

What you're looking at is the most expensive private residence in Gotham City.
Valued at fifty-eight million dollars, the complex takes up the top three floors of the famous Powers Hotel and is occupied by the Powers family patriarch, Joesph, and his wife, Maria.
The place was built during the Depression, as a fortress against the masses. It has its own wooden gymnasium, pool, bowling alley...it even has a Zeppelin moor on the balcony.
Protected by both hotel and private guards, armed with encrypted wireless security, it has never seen a visitor not employed, or invited, by the Powers family.
Until tonight.
DEAR GOD...
SECURITY!
I SAID SECURITY! HELP ME, I'M--

GOING DOWN?

YOU...YOU CAN'T BE IN HERE. I'M CALLING--
THAT... THAT'S NOT JOSEPH'S.
I KNOW, MRS. POWERS.
IT'S YOURS. I FOUND THE CASE FOR YOUR HUSBAND'S MASK, BUT IT'S EMPTY.
WHERE IS HE?
GONE. OUT OF THE COUNTRY.
AND YOU AND YOUR FRIENDS... YOU MIGHT THINK YOU HAVE THE UPPER HAND RIGHT NOW, BUT YOU DON'T!
YOU NEVER WILL!
IN...IN FACT, IF I WERE YOU, I'D LEAVE THE CITY AND NEVER COME BACK.
AND IF I WERE YOU...
...I'D GET USED TO THAT VIEW.

YOUR SCARE TACTICS WORKED, SIR. SHE'S DIALING HER HUSBAND NOW.
TELL ME YOU CAN TRACK THE CALL, ALFRED.
IT LOOKS AS THOUGH WE CAN. THOUGH HIS LINE IS BASICALLY IMPENETRABLY CODED, WE'RE NOW ABLE TO "PIGGYBACK" ON HERS TO LOCATE HIS PHONE.
AND THE TALONS?
CRYO
I MOVED THEM INTO THE COLD STORAGE LABORATORY, SIR...
...THEY SEEM TO HAVE RETREATED INTO SOME KIND OF PRESERVATORY STASIS.
GOOD.
TELL ME WHEN YOU HAVE A LOCK ON MR. POWERS.

IT'S STRANGE, SIR...
...THE PHONE APPEARS TO BE LOCATED IN SOME KIND OF BLACKOUT ZONE.
A BLACKOUT ZONE?
YES. SOMEONE HAS CREATED A DEAD AREA ABOUT A QUARTER MILE IN RADIUS. I CAN PLACE THE PHONE WITHIN THE ZONE ITSELF, BUT BEYOND THAT...
AND THE LOCATION?
...THE BLACKOUT ZONE IS LOCATED ON GOTHAM'S SOUTH SIDE, SIR.
ALONG THE ROW?
YES, AND JUDGING BY THE EMISSION FIELD, I CALCULATE THE EPICENTER TO BE SOMEWHERE AROUND--
IRVINGTON...
--I'M SORRY, SIR?
77 IRVINGTON. RIGHT WHERE IT ALWAYS WAS.
YES... BUT, HOW DID YOU KNOW, SIR?
MASTER BRUCE?

Henri Ducard, the great detective, once told me that there's a feeling you get on a case sometimes...
Earlier tonight, when Lincoln March gave me his short list of names, I felt it. I saw Joseph Powers' name on the list and I knew.
Not just because he was responsible for the founding of the Gotham Aviary, for its exceptional collection of rare owls. Not because his finances seem skewed. But because I felt it in my gut, that remembering.
And now, here, I feel it again...
...a feeling that comes when the pieces suddenly fit into place and the answer you've been looking for all that time begins to appear.
The feeling, Ducard said, is like "a remembering." Not so much a discovery of something new, as a remembering of what you knew all along. Something right in front of you.
That feeling is the best indicator you have your answer, said Ducard.
...outside this building.
I came to Harbor House when I was a boy. I was looking for the Court of Owls.
That time I found nothing.
Not tonight.

Tonight, the Court goes down. Once and for all.
No more hiding. No more plotting from the shadows.
Tonight their story **ends**. Their little song will be forgotten. Their name vanishes from Gotham's history.
They know it, too. Rushing to meet here in the middle of the night.
The report from Alfred is that many of the assassination attempts tonight were stopped. Most of the Court's Talons are down.
And now I have them cornered.
No security, no traps...**nothing** can keep me from them.

Not tonight.
Not...

...not again.
DAMN YOU...

"...DAMN YOU ALL."
MASTER BRUCE?
YOU'RE NOT DRESSED. DON'T FORGET, YOU'RE MEETING WITH THE FIRMS BIDDING ON THE ELEVATED PARK IN LESS THAN AN HOUR.
I TOLD YOU. I'M WAITING ON THE GRAY, ALFRED.
YES, WELL, IT SEEMS TO HAVE SNUCK UP ON YOU, SIR.

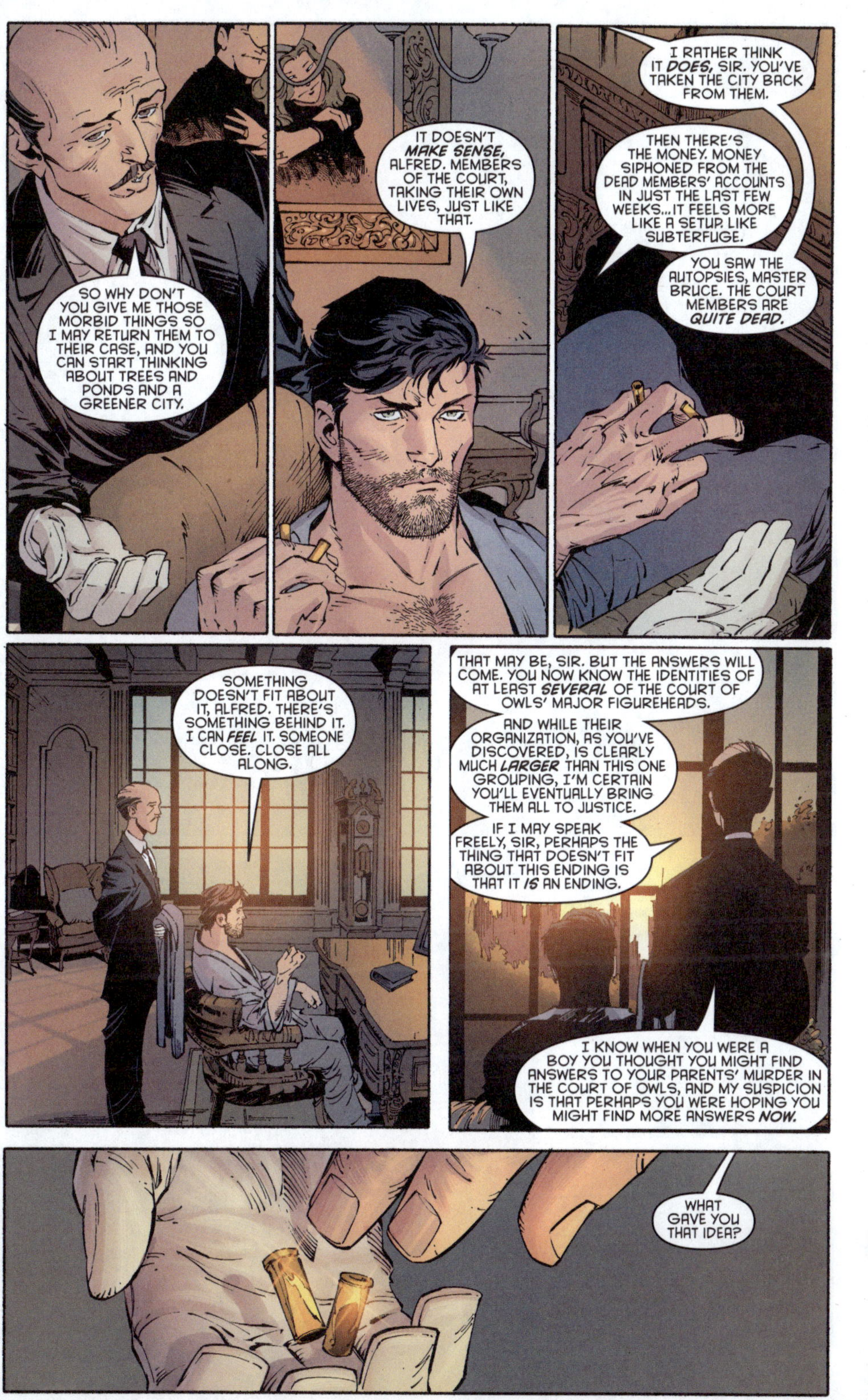
SO WHY DON'T YOU GIVE ME THOSE MORBID THINGS SO I MAY RETURN THEM TO THEIR CASE, AND YOU CAN START THINKING ABOUT TREES AND PONDS AND A GREENER CITY.
IT DOESN'T MAKE SENSE, ALFRED. MEMBERS OF THE COURT, TAKING THEIR OWN LIVES, JUST LIKE THAT.
I RATHER THINK IT DOES, SIR. YOU'VE TAKEN THE CITY BACK FROM THEM.
THEN THERE'S THE MONEY. MONEY SIPHONED FROM THE DEAD MEMBERS' ACCOUNTS IN JUST THE LAST FEW WEEKS...IT FEELS MORE LIKE A SETUP. LIKE SUBTERFUGE.
YOU SAW THE AUTOPSIES, MASTER BRUCE. THE COURT MEMBERS ARE QUITE DEAD.
SOMETHING DOESN'T FIT ABOUT IT, ALFRED. THERE'S SOMETHING BEHIND IT. I CAN FEEL IT. SOMEONE CLOSE. CLOSE ALL ALONG.
THAT MAY BE, SIR. BUT THE ANSWERS WILL COME. YOU NOW KNOW THE IDENTITIES OF AT LEAST SEVERAL OF THE COURT OF OWLS' MAJOR FIGUREHEADS.
AND WHILE THEIR ORGANIZATION, AS YOU'VE DISCOVERED, IS CLEARLY MUCH LARGER THAN THIS ONE GROUPING, I'M CERTAIN YOU'LL EVENTUALLY BRING THEM ALL TO JUSTICE.
IF I MAY SPEAK FREELY, SIR, PERHAPS THE THING THAT DOESN'T FIT ABOUT THIS ENDING IS THAT IT IS AN ENDING.
I KNOW WHEN YOU WERE A BOY YOU THOUGHT YOU MIGHT FIND ANSWERS TO YOUR PARENTS' MURDER IN THE COURT OF OWLS, AND MY SUSPICION IS THAT PERHAPS YOU WERE HOPING YOU MIGHT FIND MORE ANSWERS NOW.
WHAT GAVE YOU THAT IDEA?

WHEN IT COMES TO THEM? TO THEIR MURDER? YOU ARE THE ANSWER TO THAT MYSTERY, BRUCE WAYNE. AND THAT ANSWER...
...IS ENOUGH.
NOW PUT ON THAT BLOODY SUIT AND GET OUT OF HERE!
ALL RIGHT, ALL RIGHT. I'M GOING.
JUST CALL ROBERTS AND TELL...
...TELL HIM...
TELL HIM WHAT, SIR?
TELL HIM...
...I WON'T BE ABLE TO MAKE IT.
BUT, SIR. WHERE ARE YOU--
I'M GOING AFTER HIM, ALFRED.

"AFTER *WHO,* MASTER BRUCE?
"SIR? ...*WHO?*"
"*HIM.* THE ANSWER TO ALL THIS.
"THE ONE BEHIND IT. THE ONE I *FORGOT.*"
Follow me down the Rabbit hole?
RIGHT BEHIND YOU, OLD FRIEND.

Sinkholes are tricky things. They can form in more places than most people think.
In cities, they form particularly quickly, often exacerbated by leaky pipes and overly heavy structures.
Gotham has a sinkhole. Just one. It's the only one in Kane County, in fact.
And it sits beneath this place.
The Willowwood Home for Children.
Years ago, it was Gotham's satellite hospital for children suffering from mental illness and neurological disorders.
Death

It operated until eighteen years ago, when a sinkhole swallowed the orderlies' quarters.
In the days that followed the catastrophe, the truth about Willowwood became clear.
The abuses the children had been subjected to. The neglect. Children. Alone, naked, rotting in their filth. Left to starve.
Now, it sits abandoned, and children dare each other to spend the night inside.
They say the sadness of the lost children caused the sinkhole. They say the place is haunted by their spirits.
Tonight, I almost believe it... after all, I'm here to catch a dead man.
I'M HERE.

UNH!
SO TELL ME, BATMAN... WHO?
WHO AM I?
I DON'T KNOW. BUT YOU'RE NOT LINCOLN MARCH. BECAUSE LINCOLN MARCH DOESN'T EXIST.
HE'S A PAPER MAN, SET UP BY THE COURT OF OWLS.
GOOD. SO IF I'M NOT LINCOLN MARCH, THEN WHO AM I?

YOU'RE A TRAITOR AND A THIEF. YOU WERE A MEMBER OF THE COURT OF OWLS, BUT YOU BETRAYED THEM. JUST AS EVERYTHING WAS CRUMBLING ON THEM.
YOU TOOK MONEY FROM THE TOP MEMBERS, YOU INVITED THEM TO AN EMERGENCY COUNCIL, AND YOU POISONED THEM. YOU MADE IT LOOK LIKE THEY KILLED THEMSELVES.
MEANWHILE, YOU INCLUDED YOUR NAME ON THE LIST OF TARGETS, YOU HAD ONE OF THE TALONS COME AFTER YOU, AND YOU FAKED YOUR OWN DEATH--
NOT FAKED.
NO, NOT FAKED. YOU TOOK THE SERUM BEFORE THE ATTACK. THE COMPOUND THAT BROUGHT THE TALONS BACK TO LIFE.
THE COURT WILL COME AFTER YOU, LINCOLN. THE MEMBERS YOU KILLED WERE ONLY A SMALL HANDFUL OF--
OH THEY'LL COME AFTER ME, ALL RIGHT. BUT *HEH* I'M PRETTY DAMNED HARD TO KILL, NOW.
YOU KNOW, BRUCE, FOR A WHILE, THERE WAS TALK OF TRAINING A NEW TALON. BEFORE THE SERUM WAS DEVELOPED TO ALLOW FOR THE WAKING OF THE TALONS' PAST. THERE WAS EVEN A SUIT DEVELOPED.
SOMETHING TOUGH AND MODERN. SOMETHING TO RIVAL THE BATMAN.
BUT ALL THIS GETS AWAY FROM THE QUESTION...
...BECAUSE YOU'RE TELLING ME WHAT I DID.
NOT WHO I AM.
SO WHO, BRUCE, WHO? I KNOW YOU HAVE A THEORY.

MY THEORY? YOU WERE AN INMATE HERE AT ONE TIME.
GOOD. SO TELL ME HOW YOU YOU DEDUCED THAT.
SNIP
MEN LIKE YOU--CRIMINALS--ALWAYS LEAVE CLUES BEHIND.
NOT BECAUSE YOU'RE SLOPPY, BUT BECAUSE YOU'RE EGOTISTICAL. YOU LIKE TO TAUNT YOUR PURSUERS.
SO THE SINKHOLE. THE STORY YOU TOLD ME WHEN I VISITED YOU IN THE HOSPTIAL, AFTER WE WERE ATTACKED AT OLD WAYNE TOWER. YOU WERE DARING ME TO LOOK DEEPER INTO YOU.
YOU KNEW THE RECORDS THE COURT OF OWLS CREATED WERE TOO GOOD TO PENETRATE, BUT EVEN SO, YOU LEFT A CLUE.
A TRUTH INSIDE THE LIE.
A TRUTH INSIDE THE LIE. EXACTLY, JUST LIKE WITH YOU. LIKE WHEN I SAW YOU FIGHT THAT TALON DURING OUR FIRST MEETING. YOU WERE SUPPOSED TO BE AN EASY HIT.
THE COURT SAID I COULD BE THERE TO WATCH. AND WHEN I SAW WHAT YOU WERE...THE BATMAN...THAT'S WHEN I KNEW WHAT I HAD TO DO. WHAT I NEEDED TO BECOME.
BUT I SAW WHO THEY WERE, TOO--THE COURT. THEY SAID THE TALON ATTACKED ME BY ACCIDENT, THAT HE MADE A MISTAKE, BUT I SAW THE TRUTH IN THAT LIE, TOO.
SO WHO AM I, BRUCE? GO ON. I WAS AN INMATE HERE AS A CHILD AND THE COURT TOOK ME IN...WHY?
BECAUSE YOU WERE SOMEONE WITH NOTHING, SOMEONE THEY COULD PROP UP AND CONTROL, SOMEONE THEY COULD CREATE FROM SCRATCH. THEIR OWN CANDIDATE. LINCOLN MARCH.
NO! BECAUSE OF WHO I ALREADY WAS! WHO I AM...
YOU'RE MAKING ME ANGRY, AVOIDING THE QUESTION, BRUCE. BUT IF YOU WON'T ANSWER IT, ANSWER THIS: HOW? WHAT TIPPED YOU OFF? WHAT SENT YOU TO THE MORGUE?
...
SAY IT!

THE PIN.
THE PIN! WHAT PIN?
IN THE STORY YOU TOLD ME, IN OLD WAYNE TOWER. ABOUT YOUR MOTHER'S DEATH. THE CAR ACCIDENT THAT KILLED HER.
THERE'S THE LIE, BUT WHERE'S THE TRUTH?
YOU MENTIONED A PIN SHE WORE. A MISSHAPEN HEART PIN. MADE OF CLAY.
AND?
"YOU SAW THE PICTURE OF MY MOTHER WEARING THAT PIN AND YOU USED IT IN YOUR--"
NO. THE TRUTH IN THE LIE, BRUCE. THAT PIN. IT WAS ONLY GIVEN TO THE MOTHERS OF CHILDREN WHO LIVED HERE AT WILLOWWOOD.
SO WHO AM I, BRUCE?
WHO? I ASK, LIKE THE GREAT OWL, WHO?!
YOU'RE SICK.
YOU'RE NOTHING. YOU'RE--
YOUR BROTHER, BRUCE.
I'M THOMAS WAYNE, JR.
YOUR BROTHER THAT NEVER WAS. FROM THE OTHER SIDE OF THE MIRROR.

I DON'T HAVE A BROTHER!
OH, BUT YOU WERE SUPPOSED TO, THOUGH, REMEMBER? I KNOW YOU DO. THINK BACK, TO BEFORE. I WAS THERE, IN MOTHER'S STOMACH... BUT THERE WAS AN ACCIDENT, BRUCE. REMEMBER?
YOU WERE THERE. I WAS BORN EARLY, BORN HURT. AND OUR PARENTS HID ME HERE. AT WILLOWWOOD. TO HEAL AWAY FROM THE WORLD.
I DON'T KNOW WHAT THE HELL YOU'RE TALKING ABOUT, LINCOLN, WHAT STORY THE COURT CONCOCTED FOR YOU, BUT THAT'S THEIR MISTAKE.
MY PARENTS WOULDN'T DO THAT. THEY WOULDN'T PUT A SON OF THEIRS, SICK OR NOT, IN A PLACE LIKE THIS.
SEE, BUT IT WASN'T LIKE THIS BACK THEN, AT THE TIME OF THE ACCIDENT. IT WAS A PREMIER CHILDREN'S HOSPITAL.
THAT IS UNTIL THE FUNDING DRIED UP. WHEN THE HOSPITAL'S BIGGEST DONORS DIED. THOMAS AND MARTHA WAYNE. TRAGICALLY SHOT IN AN ALLEY.
YOU WANTED TO KNOW IF THE COURT HAD ANYTHING TO DO WITH OUR PARENTS' DEATHS, BRUCE. THE ANSWER IS NO. THEY DIDN'T. THAT WAS ALL YOUR FAULT, BROTHER.
AND I'M GOING TO MAKE YOU PAY.
SO FINISH CUTTING THROUGH THE NET. AND LET'S HAVE THIS OUT ONCE AND FOR ALL... FOR THE CITY OF GOTHAM.
WAYNE TO WAYNE.
YOU'RE OUT OF YOUR MIND...
BROTHER TO BROTHER...

OWL TO BAT!

# CHAPTER ELEVEN • MY BROTHER'S KEEPER

THAT ALL YOU GOT, BROTHER? OR ARE YOU JUST PLAYING NICE?

YOU'RE *NOT* MY BROTHER.
YOU'RE A LUNATIC IN A BIRD SUIT...
...AND I WAS DONE PLAYING NICE...
...A LONG TIME AGO!
IS IT *MY TURN* NOW?
GOOD.

IT'S A STORY AS OLD AS MAN, BRUCE. TWO BROTHERS. SONS OF A FABLED LINE.
LIKE ROMULUS AND REMUS! ETEOCLES AND POLYNICES! BRUCE AND THOMAS, SONS OF GOTHAM. MEANT TO SHARE THE CITY!
SKINNT
BUT ONE BROTHER ALWAYS GETS GREEDY AND TAKES IT ALL IN THOSE STORIES, DOESN'T HE?
HE TAKES THE CITY FOR HIS OWN AND FORGETS HIS KIN.
LEAVES HIS FALLEN BROTHER TO ROT. JUST LIKE YOU DID.

WELL, THIS TIME THE STORY HAS A *TWIST ENDING,* BRUCE! BECAUSE THIS TIME THE FALLEN BROTHER *WINS* IN THE END!
ALL RIGHT, LINCOLN...
...YOU WANT TO BE MY FALLEN BROTHER SO BAD...
*...THEN START FALLING!*

YOU'VE HAD YOUR GOTHAM FOR SO LONG NOW...LET ME SHOW YOU MINE! THE CITY I KNEW, FROM MY BED AT WILLOWWOOD!
-KOFF- OKAY, YOU WANT TO SPEND A LITTLE MORE TIME TOGETHER FIRST? I'M GLAD! LET'S DO IT!
FIRST, THE CROWNE TOWER! NOTHING SPECIAL TO MOST PEOPLE, JUST AN OFFICE BUILDING!
BUT ON CLEAR DAYS, FROM MY BED, I COULD SEE WAYNE INDUSTRIES IN THE REFLECTION!
PFFT
UH-UH. NO WAY OFF THE TOUR BUS NOW, BROTHER!
TAKE A CLOSE LOOK! SEE THE KINGDOM AS I DID EVERY DAY, REVERSED AND UNNATURAL...

...WELCOME TO THE OTHER SIDE OF THE MIRROR, BRUCE!
NOW LIVE AS I DID! RIGHT FROM THE START!
FEEL YOURSELF BEING BORN AGAIN AS ME IN THAT CAR CRASH. YOU'RE LIKE A BIRD DROPPED FROM THE NEST, SMASHED AWAKE!
NOW YOU'RE A CHILD, YOU'RE GROWING, BUT YOU'RE BROKEN. SOMETHING IS WRONG. YOU CAN'T MOVE, CAN'T TALK.
YOU CAN SEE, THOUGH, THROUGH THE BAREST OF SLITS BETWEEN YOUR EYELIDS...YOU WATCH.
EVERYONE THINKS YOU'RE ASLEEP INSIDE. THEY'RE WAITING FOR YOU TO DIE... EVERY DAY YOU'RE SUPPOSED TO! BUT YOU DON'T...
...BECAUSE YOU'RE ALIVE IN THERE! YOU'RE AWAKE! YOU DON'T EVEN KNOW WHO YOU ARE, BUT YOU'RE SOMEONE! YOU FEEL IT!
WHO, THOUGH? WHO?
AND THERE'S THE WOMAN. SHE COMES OFTEN. SHE SITS ON YOUR BED. YOU KNOW SHE'S YOUR MOTHER, SHE'S THE KEY!
BUT YOU CAN'T CALL TO HER, CAN'T MOVE!

AND THEN ONE DAY, SHE'S ON THE TELEVISION IN YOUR ROOM. AND YOU KNOW!
A REVELATION! SUDDENLY YOU KNOW WHO YOU ARE, BECAUSE THE OWLS ARE THERE NOW, TOO. WHISPERING TO YOU AT NIGHT.
TELLING YOU WHAT YOU ALREADY KNEW ALL ALONG-- THAT YOU'RE THOMAS WAYNE, JR. A SON OF THE CITY!
YOUR PARENTS ARE GONE, BUT YOUR BROTHER! YOUR BROTHER IS STILL OUT THERE!
AND YOU THINK TO YOURSELF, HE'LL COME FOR ME, WON'T HE? HE'LL COME FOR ME...
YOU WAIT EVERY DAY, ALL DAY, THE OWLS WHISPERING AS THE HOUSE AROUND YOU GOES TO HELL.
BUT HE DOESN'T COME. ONLY THE OWLS COME, AND SOON ENOUGH, THEY SAVE YOU FROM THAT PLACE, THEY START TO HELP YOU HEAL, FIX YOUR MIND.
STILL YOU WAIT FOR YOUR BROTHER... HE MUST REMEMBER YOU! YOU KNOW HE DOES! BUT ALL YOU HEAR IS THE TIME PASSING. THE BIG CHURCH BELL RINGING... BONG! BONG! BONG!
BONG

SO YOU FINALLY ACCEPT IT. YOU ACCEPT THAT YOUR BROTHER HAS FORCED YOU OUT OF HIS MIND SO HE CAN HAVE IT ALL--THE WHOLE CITY. AND YOU ACCEPT THAT THIS REVERSE CITY IS YOURS...
THE ONE YOUR BROTHER EXILED YOU TO, A PALE REFLECTION, A BACKWARDS CITY THAT PEOPLE ENTER BUT NEVER LEAVE. A GOTHAM THAT TRAPS YOU IN PLACE!
I MEAN THAT LITERALLY, BRUCE! SEE THE GOTHAM AIRPORT OVER THERE? THE RUNWAYS ARE ALL DIRECTED EAST FOR TAKE-OFF AND WEST FOR LANDING!
SO ALL DAY I HEARD PLANES COMING, NEVER LEAVING. NEVER EVER LEAVING...
AND SO ENDS OUR TOUR, BROTHER!
I'LL WATCH THE PIECES OF YOU COME OUT THE OTHER SIDE, SCATTERED OVER THE CITY YOU THOUGHT YOU KNEW SO WELL...
...BUT DIDN'T KNOW AT ALL!

IT'S OKAY, BRUCE! YOU CAN *LET GO* NOW!
YOUR BROTHER IS WATCHING OVER YOU. JUST AS HE *ALWAYS* HAS.

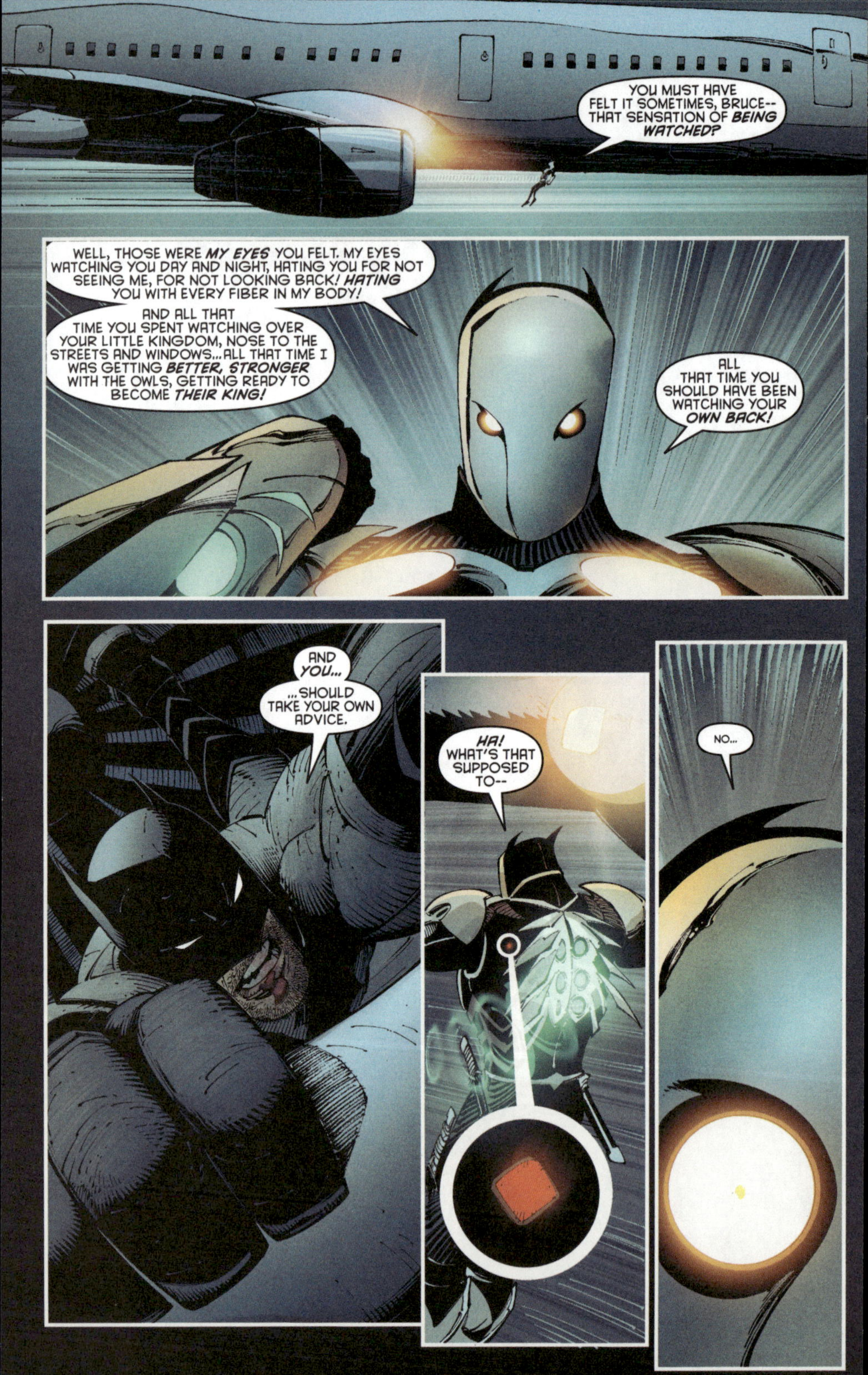
YOU MUST HAVE FELT IT SOMETIMES, BRUCE-- THAT SENSATION OF *BEING WATCHED?*
WELL, THOSE WERE *MY EYES* YOU FELT. MY EYES WATCHING YOU DAY AND NIGHT, HATING YOU FOR NOT SEEING ME, FOR NOT LOOKING BACK! *HATING* YOU WITH EVERY FIBER IN MY BODY!
AND ALL THAT TIME YOU SPENT WATCHING OVER YOUR LITTLE KINGDOM, NOSE TO THE STREETS AND WINDOWS...ALL THAT TIME I WAS GETTING *BETTER, STRONGER* WITH THE OWLS, GETTING READY TO BECOME *THEIR KING!*
ALL THAT TIME YOU SHOULD HAVE BEEN WATCHING YOUR *OWN BACK!*
AND *YOU...*
...SHOULD TAKE YOUR OWN ADVICE.
*HA!* WHAT'S THAT SUPPOSED TO--
NO...

Suit... dead.
Nothing left. No power.
Can't hold on any longer...

Nothing to hold on to...
...not anymore.
She looks so beautiful from up here.
Dick...you always liked taking the plane.
Seeing the city this way...
...I see why.
I try to let go...
...but even as I do...
...the city...
...she calls me back to her.
She saves me.
She reminds me...we still have work to do.
SWITCH TO HIGH VELOCITY BAT-ROPE, NOW!

UNH!
YOU JUST WON'T STAY DEAD--WILL YOU, BROTHER?

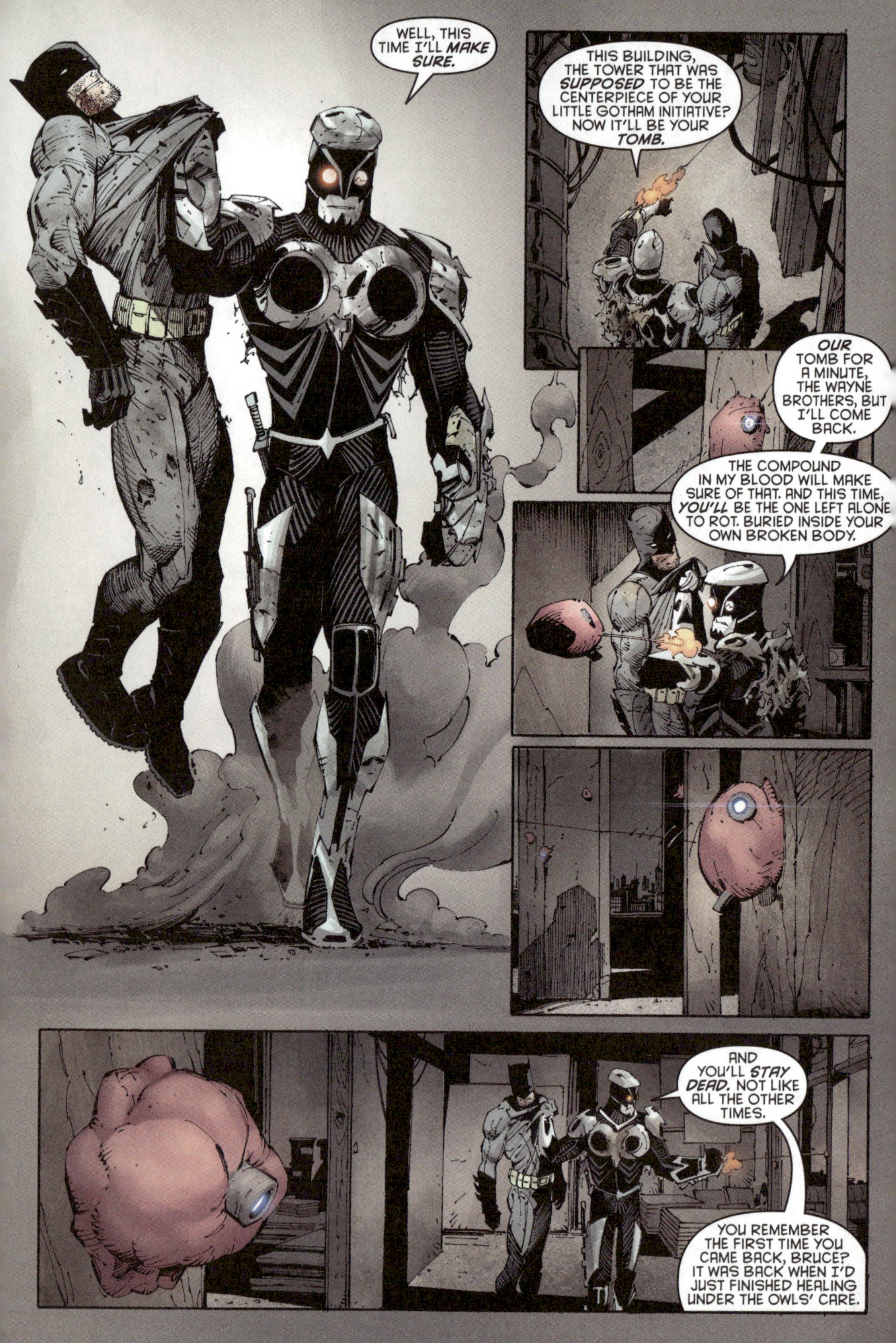
WELL, THIS TIME I'LL MAKE SURE.
THIS BUILDING, THE TOWER THAT WAS SUPPOSED TO BE THE CENTERPIECE OF YOUR LITTLE GOTHAM INITIATIVE? NOW IT'LL BE YOUR TOMB.
OUR TOMB FOR A MINUTE, THE WAYNE BROTHERS, BUT I'LL COME BACK.
THE COMPOUND IN MY BLOOD WILL MAKE SURE OF THAT. AND THIS TIME, YOU'LL BE THE ONE LEFT ALONE TO ROT. BURIED INSIDE YOUR OWN BROKEN BODY.
AND YOU'LL STAY DEAD. NOT LIKE ALL THE OTHER TIMES.
YOU REMEMBER THE FIRST TIME YOU CAME BACK, BRUCE? IT WAS BACK WHEN I'D JUST FINISHED HEALING UNDER THE OWLS' CARE.

YOU'D BEEN GONE FOR YEARS. YOU'D LEFT TO TRAVEL THE WORLD...
...AND YOU DISAPPEARED. THE COURT HAD SAID YOU DIED SOMEWHERE IN THE HIMALAYAS, OR THE BACK ALLEYS OF PARIS.
I WAS HEALED, AND THE OWLS' PLAN WAS TO PRESENT ME TO THE CITY AS MYSELF, AS THOMAS WAYNE, JR. I WAS GOING TO BRING THE HOUSE OF WAYNE TO ITS GREATEST HEIGHTS, WITH THEIR HELP.
BUT THEN... YOU RETURNED. OUT OF NOWHERE.
AND THE COURT THOUGHT THE SPOTLIGHT ON THE WAYNE FAMILY WAS TOO BRIGHT...
SO THEY CAME UP WITH "LINCOLN MARCH," A MAN I COULD BECOME TO RECLAIM THE CITY FOR THEM IN A DIFFERENT WAY. "YOU'LL BE THE BEAK OF THE GREAT OWL," THEY SAID.
BUT THAT'S NOT WHAT I WANTED, BRUCE. I WANTED THE CITY IN EARNEST. IT WAS MY TIME.
NOW I CAN NEVER HAVE IT. I KNOW THAT. BUT IF I CAN'T BE THIS CITY'S FUTURE, I'LL BE ITS SECRET PAST...
...I'LL BE THE PAST COME TO GET YOU. THE GOTHAM OF THE DEAD, THE GHOST CITY. ALL THE ONES YOU NEVER LOOKED BACK AT IN YOUR ARROGANCE. I'LL STAND FOR THEM.
SO DIE KNOWING THIS, BROTHER. YOU? YOU'RE NOTHING BUT A FOOTNOTE, A BLIP, DESTINED TO BE FORGOTTEN.
ME, I AM GOTHAM'S HISTORY!
FINALLY *KOFF*...

...SOMETHING WE AGREE ON!
AAGGH!
RUN, BRUCE! RUN FROM THE TRUTH!
RUN LIKE YOU ALWAYS HAVE...
"...BUT WHEN YOU FEEL THAT PRICKLING ON THE BACK OF YOUR NECK, KNOW THAT I'M COMING FOR YOU!
"REACHING FOR YOU FROM THE OTHER SIDE OF YOUR REFLECTION!"

"THE WHOLE TOWER WAS DESTROYED, DOWN TO ITS FOUNDATION.
"I CONDUCTED A SEARCH PRIVATELY AND CAME UP EMPTY, TOO.
"NO CASUALTIES.
"NO BODIES FOUND IN THE WRECKAGE AT ALL."

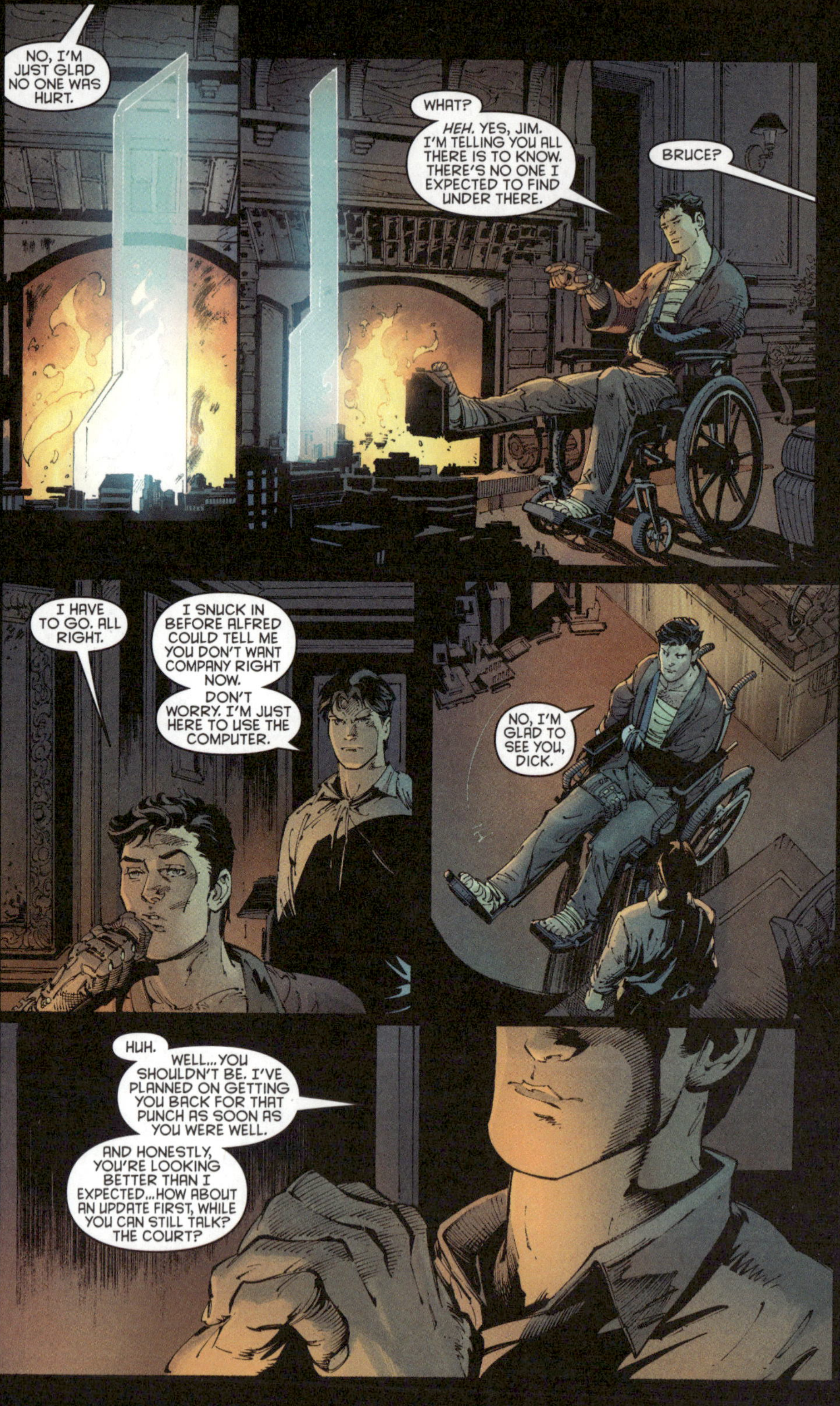

NO, I'M JUST GLAD NO ONE WAS HURT.
WHAT?
HEH. YES, JIM. I'M TELLING YOU ALL THERE IS TO KNOW. THERE'S NO ONE I EXPECTED TO FIND UNDER THERE.
BRUCE?
I HAVE TO GO. ALL RIGHT.
I SNUCK IN BEFORE ALFRED COULD TELL ME YOU DON'T WANT COMPANY RIGHT NOW.
DON'T WORRY. I'M JUST HERE TO USE THE COMPUTER.
NO, I'M GLAD TO SEE YOU, DICK.
HUH.
WELL...YOU SHOULDN'T BE. I'VE PLANNED ON GETTING YOU BACK FOR THAT PUNCH AS SOON AS YOU WERE WELL.
AND HONESTLY, YOU'RE LOOKING BETTER THAN I EXPECTED...HOW ABOUT AN UPDATE FIRST, WHILE YOU CAN STILL TALK? THE COURT?

"I'M STILL MAKING INROADS, FOLLOWING THE MONEY. BUT THE TRUTH IS, THEIR RESOURCES ARE *STAGGERING.* AND THE MAZE THEY'VE MADE TO HIDE THEIR TRAIL...WITHOUT A DOUBT, THEY'RE STILL OUT THERE...
"...BUT THEY'RE HURTING. AND I'LL MAKE SURE THEY *KEEP* HURTING UNTIL I FIND THEM ALL...
"...AND WASH AWAY THE STAIN OF THE COURT ALTOGETHER."
"AND THE CAPTURED TALONS?"
"I'VE HAD THEM MOVED TO A CRYO-PRISON BENEATH BLACKGATE. WAYNE FUNDED, OF COURSE.
"AS FOR THE ONES WHO GOT AWAY, WE'LL FIND THEM SOON ENOUGH."
OF COURSE WE WILL. JUST A MATTER OF TIME.
I'LL BE SEEING YOU, BRUCE.
DICK, WAIT...
I ASSUME ALFRED TOLD YOU ABOUT LINCOLN MARCH'S CLAIMS?

HE DID. BUT WITH HOW THINGS HAVE BEEN BETWEEN US LATELY...HONESTLY, I DIDN'T WANT TO PRY.
NO. I'D LIKE YOU TO KNOW.
THERE WAS ANOTHER WAYNE CHILD...
...I WAS THREE WHEN MY MOTHER WAS PREGNANT WITH...HIM. WE WERE IN A CAR ACCIDENT TOGETHER. I DON'T...I DON'T REMEMBER THE ACCIDENT. BUT THERE'S A RECORD.
THE CHILD WAS BORN PREMATURE, WITH NEUROLOGICAL DAMAGE. SEVERE ENOUGH THAT HE WOULD HAVE REMAINED IN A PERMANENT VEGETATIVE STATE HAD HE LIVED THROUGH THE INITIAL TRAUMA.
HE DIDN'T LIVE, THOUGH?
HE DID...
...FOR A SINGLE NIGHT.

HOSPITAL RECORDS AT GOTHAM MERCY SUGGEST HE WAS BORN UNDER DURESS, NAMED, AND IMMEDIATELY INTUBATED.
HE DIED TWELVE HOURS LATER.
BUT FOR ONE NIGHT, HERE IN GOTHAM, I *DID* HAVE A BROTHER.
FORGIVE ME, BRUCE, BUT...PLAYING DEVILS' ADVOCATE, IS IT IN ANY WAY POSSIBLE THAT YOUR BROTHER--
SURVIVED THAT FIRST NIGHT AT MERCY? AND THAT AFTERWARDS MY PARENTS SECRETLY MOVED HIM TO WILLOWWOOD FOR TREATMENT? ARE YOU ASKING IF I THINK THEY COULD HAVE *FALSIFIED* THE RECORDS?
THEN THE ANSWER IS *NO.* I DON'T BELIEVE THEY COULD. I INVESTIGATED THE MERCY RECORDS FROM ALL ANGLES, AND THERE'S NO SIGN THEY WERE FALSIFIED.
GOOD. SO YOU HAVE YOUR ANSWER. AND YOU CAN MOVE ON.
I WAS *ALSO* ABLE TO DIG UP SOME OF THE ORIGINAL PENCIL AND PAPER RECORDS FROM WILLOWWOOD, AND THERE WAS A JOHN DOE, A BABY, ADMITTED ABOUT A WEEK AFTER THOMAS WAS SUPPOSED TO HAVE DIED.
THE RECORDS ALSO SHOW THAT MY MOTHER VISITED THE HOSPITAL OFTEN.
BUT SHE VISITED *EVERY* CHARITY SHE FUNDED OFTEN. THE HEART PIN COULD EASILY HAVE BEEN HONORARY.
ALL OF THIS IS EVIDENCE THE COURT WOULD HAVE USED TO *CONVINCE* LINCOLN HE WAS MY BROTHER.
BUT IN THE END, IF WHAT YOU'RE ASKING IS WHETHER IT'S POSSIBLE THAT LINCOLN'S STORY IS TRUE...
...ALL I CAN SAY IS THAT WITHOUT HIS *DNA,* I CAN'T KNOW FOR SURE.
HELL, THERE'S NO WAY TO KNOW IF LINCOLN'S CLAIM TO BE THOMAS WASN'T PART OF THE COURT'S PLAN. MAYBE THEY SACRIFICED SOME MEMBERS THEMSELVES AND PUT HIM UP TO IT. TO THROW ME OFF THEIR TRAIL, OR BUY TIME.
IT'S STILL A MYSTERY, FOR NOW.

AND YOU'RE ALL RIGHT WITH THAT?
NO. I'M NOT. BUT I SUPPOSE IN THIS CITY I *HAVE* TO BE.
WELL THAT'S VERY BIG OF Y--
UNTIL I FIND THAT EVIDENCE.
THE COURT OF OWLS TRIED TO UNDERMINE EVERYTHING I BELIEVE IN, BUT ONE THING THEY COULD NEVER MAKE ME QUESTION IS MY BELIEF IN MY PARENTS. IF THOMAS, JR. HAD LIVED PAST THAT ONE NIGHT, THEY'D HAVE *TOLD* ME.
THEY WOULD HAVE. I KNOW IT.
I BELIEVE WHAT YOU BELIEVE, BRUCE. BUT STILL...
IF THOMAS WAS NEVER SUPPOSED TO RECOVER, I MEAN IF IT WAS HOPELESS...
LOOK, ALL I'M SAYING IS THAT SOMETIMES, PROTECTING THE PEOPLE YOU CARE ABOUT FROM A PAINFUL TRUTH AND CARRYING IT AS A PRIVATE PAIN INSTEAD...I NOW SEE THAT IT CAN BE A *NOBLE* THING, YOU KNOW?
...
DICK, LISTEN. I KNOW IT MUST HAVE BEEN HARD, FINDING OUT THAT YOU WERE MEANT TO BE A TALON, TO BE ONE OF THE OWLS.
WELL THANK YOU, B--
I'M NOT DONE.
I KNOW IT MIGHT SEEM LIKE I SAVED YOU FROM THAT DESTINY. BUT YOU COULD NEVER HAVE BEEN ONE OF THEM. *NEVER.* THEY MIGHT HAVE SEEN SOMETHING IN YOU, BACK THEN. BUT SO DID I.
AND THE TRUTH IS, I DIDN'T SAVE YOU FROM SOME DARK FATE, THOSE YEARS AGO. YOU SAVED *ME* FROM ONE.
AND YOU STILL ARE SAVING ME, EVERY DAY.
...
*SIGH* DAMMIT, BRUCE. NOW I CAN'T HIT YOU. I'LL JUST HAVE TO DO IT SOME OTHER TIME. IT'S FINE, THOUGH. I'LL JUST SNEAK UP AND SURPRISE YOU.
YOU'LL TRY.

SO YOU GOING TO REBUILD?
THE TOWER? I AM. *TALLER.* IN FACT, I'M REDOUBLING MY EFFORTS WITH THE INITIATIVE.
WELL, IT'S NICE TO KNOW THAT THE OWLS DIDN'T SCARE BRUCE WAYNE BACK INTO HIS CAVE.
THE OPPOSITE, ACTUALLY. IT'S STRANGE, DICK. LATELY, RIGHT UP UNTIL ALL THIS WITH THE COURT, I'D COME TO THINK OF THE CITY AS MINE. AS BATMAN'S.
EVEN WITH THE INITIATIVE, PART OF ME WAS DOING IT TO HAVE MORE LOOKOUTS. MORE BASES FOR BATMAN RATHER THAN FOR THE CITY ITSELF. BUT I SEE NOW THAT I WAS *WRONG.*
BECAUSE GOTHAM ISN'T BATMAN.
GOTHAM ISN'T THE OWLS.
GOTHAM IS...
GOTHAM IS *ALL* OF US.
IT'S A *LITTLE* BIT BATMAN. COME ON.
IN THE END, I HAVE TO SAY I'M GRATEFUL TO THE COURT OF OWLS FOR THE LESSON. BUT EVEN SO, IF THEY REEMERGE... *WHEN* THEY REEMERGE...

...I'LL BE WATCHING. ALWAYS.
THE END

# BATMAN THE COURT OF OWLS

ADDITIONAL STORIES

## THE CALL

written by Scott Snyder & James Tynion IV

art by Rafael Albuquerque

color by Nathan Fairbairn

## THE FALL OF THE HOUSE OF WAYNE

written by Scott Snyder & James Tynion IV

art by Rafael Albuquerque

color by Dave McCaig

NIGHT OF THE OWLS, 7:32 PM...
LOOK AT THIS, FRIENDS.
BRUCE CAME OUT TO PLAY!
YOU KNOW WHAT WE DO TO BATS, BRUCE? WE EAT THEM WHOLE. BONES AND ALL.
NOT IN THIS CAVE YOU DON'T.
MASTER BRUCE...
...I'VE UPLOADED THE MATERIAL, BUT THE FIREW--
WAIT.

THIS CAN'T BE RIGHT.
WHAT IS IT, ALFRED?
MY GOD...
ALFRED?
GOTHAM CITY COMPTROLLER -- BETTY PARK
GOTHAM CITY DEPUTY SHERIFF -- MICHAEL D. DAVIS
KANE COUNTY SUPREME COURT JUSTICE -- JAN SPITZ
GOTHAM PUBLIC ADVOCATE -- JOHN LEE
SPEAKER OF THE CITY COUNCIL -- MIGUEL GUADALUPE
HEAD OF THE CITY PLANNING COMMISSION -- BILL KEEP
GOTHAM COMMISSIONER OF CULTURAL AFFAIRS -- VALERIE VENDERMAN
GOTHAM CITY POLICE COMMISSIONER -- JIM GORDON
52ND ADJUTANT GENERAL OF GOTHAM -- MAJ. GEN. BENJAMIN BURROWS
ARKHAM ASYLUM HEAD AND DIRECTOR -- JEREMIAH ARKHAM
SEBASTIAN HADY
THOMAS KAVANAUGH
RANDAL DAVIS
LINCOLN MARCH
VICTOR FRIES
IT'S A LIST, SIR.
A LIST OF WHAT?
IT'S A LIST OF TARGETS.
AND... NEARLY EVERY PUBLIC FIGURE IN GOTHAM CITY IS ON IT.

"EVERYONE WHO SHAPES THE CITY."
"THE CITY COMPTROLLER..."
BETTY PARK...

"GOTHAM CITY DEPUTY SHERIFF..."
MICHAEL D. DAVIS...
PLEASE DON'T...

"KANE COUNTY SUPREME COURT JUSTICE..."
JAN SPITZ...
"GOTHAM PUBLIC ADVOCATE..."
"THE HEAD OF THE CITY PLANNING COMMISSION..."
BILL KEEP...
"GOTHAM'S COMMISSIONER OF CULTURAL AFFAIRS..."
VALERIE VENDERMAN. THE COURT OF OWLS...

JOHN LEE...
"SPEAKER OF THE CITY COUNCIL..."
MIGUEL GUADALUPE...
...HAS SENTENCED YOU...
...TO DIE.

COMMISSIONER GORDON... MAYOR HADY... THEY'RE GOING TO KILL THEM *ALL.*
GOTHAM CITY MAYOR - SEBASTIAN HADY
GOTHAM CITY DEPUTY MAYOR - THOMAS KAVANAUGH
GOTHAM CITY COUNCILMAN - RANDAL DAVIS
GOTHAM CITY MAYORAL CANDIDATE - LINCOLN MARCH
PREMIER GOTHAM SCIENTIST - VICTOR FRIES
CEO OF WAYNE ENTERPRISES - LUCIUS FOX
PROPRIETOR OF THE ICEBERG CASINO AND LOUNGE - OSWALD COBBLEPOT
PUT OUT THE CALL, ALFRED.
ALFRED!
I'M HERE, SIR.
PUT THE CALL OUT TO THE FAMILY.
NOW.
YES... YES OF COURSE, SIR.
PUTTING IT OUT NOW.

TO ALL THE ALLIES OF THE BAT PRESENTLY IN GOTHAM...
...I SEND THIS WITH THE GREATEST URGENCY.
TONIGHT, THE COURT OF OWLS HAS SENT THEIR ASSASSINS TO KILL NEARLY FORTY PEOPLE ACROSS THE CITY.
THE COURT'S TARGETS ARE ALL GOTHAM LEADERS. PEOPLE WHO SHAPE THIS CITY.

I HAVE UPLOADED A LIST OF THE TARGETS' NAMES, HERE.
THE COURT'S ASSASSINS, THE "TALONS," ARE ALREADY EN ROUTE TO THEIR TARGETS.
THEY ARE HIGHLY TRAINED KILLERS--
--WITH EXTRAORDINARY REGENERATIVE ABILITIES.
FOR MANY OF THEIR TARGETS, I FEAR IT MAY BE TOO LATE TO--
BANG! BANG!

I WILL KEEP THE--
BANG! BANG!
--KEEP THE LINE TO THE CAVE OPEN AS LONG AS I CAN MANAGE.
BANG! BANG!
COME ON! I'M RIGHT HERE!
BANG! BANG!
WE'RE COMING FOR YOU, TOO, OLD MAN!
GOING TO TEAR THE SKIN OFF YOUR BACK!
GOOD LUCK TO YOU...
NOW! TAKE HIM!
...GOD HELP US ALL.
THE END

YEARS AGO...
From the desk of Jarvis Pennyworth:
To My Dear Son, Alfred...
FOR ALFRED
...shadows move within Wayne Manor, and I fear that I may no longer be safe.
But frightened as I am for myself, I am more frightened for you, Alfred.
Should I not survive the journey home to Britain, it is imperative that you read what I have to say...

You've long known that it is your duty to fulfill my role with the Waynes upon my retirement or passing.
I know you believe that I want this for you.
And I did, Alfred, for a long time, I did. But no longer.
I implore you, Dear Son. If you take only one line from this hurried letter, let it be this...
...never come to this house.
Never.
For you see, there's a secret to the House of Wayne, known only to those who have served the family.
And that secret is this, Alfred...this family, this house, the very ground I now walk is cursed.

If only I had seen it sooner, Alfred. If only I'd understood.
But I was blind.
Or blinded, rather...blinded by the grandeur of the Waynes, by the storied history of their line.
I couldn't see the darker legacy, the shadows behind the portraits.
Or the danger...

...the terrible danger.
I SEE YOU...
SKREEEEE
KRACK
...I SEE YOU, JARVIS PENNYWORTH...

"...AND I'M COMING FOR YOU, OLD MAN."
To think I may never see you again, Alfred. Never see you laugh or perform on the stage. Never see you marry. Or raise children of your own.
COME ON, YOU BLOODY...
CHKK
It's more than I can bear. I cannot tell you, Son, how I regret not seeing more of you these last few years.
Please know that I thought of you often.
And in my own mind, in my heart, I believed that all the effort, all the time spent serving Martha and Thomas Wayne and their young son...

...that all of it was for you, Alfred.
For I was convinced that in doing my best to serve, to help in my own way to improve this home and this family, I was making a better future for you.
Especially when it came to young Master Wayne, whom I knew you would one day serve.
I loved and cared for him so that he would one day care for you.
At least this is what I believed, then...
...perhaps I was lying to myself, though, Alfred. Perhaps I simply lost myself in the happiness of those days. That young family.
But they were happy times, my Son. Know that, too.

For a while, at least.
I'VE HAD IT, THOMAS.
THE MAYOR HAS SHUT DOWN ANOTHER *FIVE SCHOOLS,* THAT CORRUPT, SHORT-SIGHTED IDIOT...
...YOU KNOW IT'S ONLY BECAUSE THE SCHOOLS HAVEN'T FIGURED OUT A WAY TO PAY HIM OFF. IT'S *DISGUSTING.*
WELL, HE'LL GET AN EARFUL THE NEXT TIME HE COMES KNOCKING AT OUR DOOR FOR FUNDRAISING.

WE NEED TO DO *MORE* THAN THAT, THOMAS. IT'S TIME. YOU KNOW IT, TOO.
I WANT GOTHAM TO BE A PLACE THAT ANY SON OF OURS WOULD BE *PROUD* TO CALL HOME.
WHAT DO YOU THINK, JARVIS? TIME FOR US ALL TO VENTURE OUT OF THE NEST?
A FINE IDEA, MADAM.
How wrong we were, though, my Son...
I hesitate as I write this, because the temptation to blame all that followed on Martha Wayne is incredibly powerful.

And particularly since I am writing this to you, my Son, I am ashamed to tell the truth.
You see, what happened to the Waynes--and whatever might happen to me--is entirely my own fault.
KRASH
LOCKED? BUT HOW...
There is the cold hard truth, my boy.
It is I who...
NO...

...it is I who have doomed us all.

The hour is late, my boy...my Alfred.
If I do not escape soon, I fear I will never leave these wretched grounds.
Death's shadow draws closer with every passing moment.
I fear for my life, but more for the secret horrors I have unleashed...
AAHHH!
...not only upon the Lady Martha and Master Thomas...

...but the very legacy of the Wayne Family.
You see, Martha had resolved herself to the creation of a new school for Gotham's underprivileged, its forgotton children.
She believed that through this school, she could shape the city into something brighter for young Master Bruce...
crayo
rayon kit - 2
...and for her second child, who was nearly due to be born.
JARVIS
Even at three years old, Bruce was an an exceptional child. Smart and kind...I knew you would love him one day as I do.
But now, none of that will come to pass.
I spent my days caring for Bruce as his mother tended to her plans and to her pregnancy.
"JARVIS, CAN YOU COME IN HERE FOR A MOMENT?"

YES, MADAM?
GATHER UP BRUCE AND GET HIM READY FOR BED. I'LL BE UP JUST AFTER THIS CALL.
I'M SORRY, MR. MAYOR, I--NO--I BEG YOUR PARDON, SIR! THESE MEN SAID THEY REPRESENTED THE CITY. WHO THE HELL ELSE WOULD I THINK--
YOU DON'T APPRECIATE *MY TONE?!*
THESE MEN THREATENED MY *UNBORN CHILD!* IF THEY CALL AGAIN, I PROMISE THAT THE LAWYERS OF BOTH THE KANE AND WAYNE FAMILIES WILL COME DOWN ON YOU SO FAST YOUR HEAD WILL SPIN.
HOW DOES *THAT* SOUND TO YOU?
RUN UP TO YOUR ROOM, NOW, MASTER BRUCE.
SLAM
JUST *LET* THEM TRY TO STOP ME.

In a city like Gotham, there will always be those who stand firmly against progress.
SMASH
My entire life, I had heard rumors, rhymes, and deadly superstitions of such figures.
My father even told me once never to push a Wayne towards greatness. Happiness is a more worthy goal.
And far less deadly.
I never took the admonition seriously, until the day I received that fateful call.

BBBRRRING
WAYNE MANOR. JARVIS SPEAKING. HOW MAY I HELP YOU?
AH! MR. PENNYWORTH. JUST THE MAN I WISHED TO REACH. I NEED YOU TO LISTEN VERY CAREFULLY.
THE NEXT TIME YOU TAKE MRS. WAYNE INTO THE CITY, YOU WILL TAKE HER TO DOCK SEVENTEEN AT THE GOTHAM MARINA, FOR A CONVERSATION BETWEEN FRIENDS.
WHY WOULD I EVER--
FAIL TO COMPLY, AND I PROMISE YOU...IT WON'T BE PLEASANT. FOR YOU OR YOUR MASTERS, PAST, PRESENT AND FUTURE.
WHO IS THIS? WHO THE HELL DO YOU THINK--
THUMP
"MADAM, I'VE JUST RECEIVED A CALL, A THREATENING CALL."

THE MAYOR'S GOONS STILL WANT TO FRIGHTEN ME, DO THEY? I THINK THEY'LL FIND I DON'T SCARE EASY.
I HAVE A SUSPICION THIS MIGHT BE BIGGER THAN CITY HALL. THEY WANT ME TO TAKE YOU TO SOME UNWATCHED CORNER OF THE DOCKS...
WELL, I GUESS WE'RE NOT GOING TO THE DOCKS THEN, ARE WE?
NO, OF COURSE NOT, MADAM.
BUT IN YOUR CONDITION, I STILL MUST URGE CAUTION--
JARVIS. IN MY "CONDITION" OR NOT, I WILL NOT BE TERRORIZED IN MY OWN CITY. NOW LET'S GET THE CAR READY. I'VE PROMISED BRUCE I'D SHOW HIM THE GROUNDS FOR THE NEW SCHOOL.
I'M BRAVE, MOMMY!
YOU'RE THE BRAVEST BOY IN GOTHAM, BRUCE. ALWAYS WILL BE.

Martha's hope and purity of spirit pushed me to agree. But I knew, in my heart, I should have insisted that we stay home.
I had my suspicions, now, as to what figures haunted the Waynes.
The Owl in the window had sealed my dread.
I could hear that silly rhyme growing louder in the back of my head, the closer we got to the school grounds.
The closer we got to that damned intersection...
SKREEEEEEE
...on the corner of Lincoln and March.
2012

Screeching metal, burning rubber and fire...followed by perfect blackness.
A blackness punctuated by the screams of the injured Martha Wayne...
...that's what I remember of that terrible night, Alfred.
The screams...and the blood. Mine, hers, Bruce's... on my face, my hands.
Oh, my boy... the blood.

Lady Martha had taken the brunt of the crash, shielding young Bruce from danger, and the trauma of the accident had caused the early birth, and loss, of her unborn child.
The days following the crash were the blackest...Martha was so consumed by sadness.
One night I actually overheard her whispering to Master Thomas as though their unborn son was still alive. When she saw me approach, she seemed horrified at her own words.
To honor their lost baby, and perhaps to expedite a healing, the Waynes planted a willow tree on the edge of the Wayne Cemetery...
...so he might look over the family for generations to come.
But the tree brought no closure for any of us. And so Master Thomas decided it would be best if they left the country for the summer. So they might heal away from the city.
As I helped him pack his belongings, I wished deep in my heart that I could simply forget the trauma of these days like young Master Bruce...
...that I could reclaim the sheer joy of life I had experienced just a few short months ago.
But the back of my mind itched with the original threat that sent us out on the road that fateful afternoon.

And when the phone rang a second time this evening, I knew who would be on the line.
BBBRIIINNG
BBRIING
YOU DIDN'T GO WHERE WE TOLD YOU, MR. PENNYWORTH, BUT WE STILL TOOK WHAT WE WANTED... THE SCHOOL IS GONE, AND A LITTLE WAYNE, TOO... HEH...
NOW THAT OUR LARGER WORK IS DONE, THE EYES OF THE OWLS HAVE TURNED TOWARD YOU.
WHAT DO YOU MEAN?!
JARVIS PENNYWORTH... WE ARE A POWERFUL ENEMY TO HAVE IN GOTHAM. NOT JUST FOR YOU, BUT FOR THOSE YOU LOVE. YOUR OWN FAMILY. YOUR SON... ALFRED...
YOU... YOU LEAVE MY SON ALONE, YOU MONSTERS! YOU HEAR ME?!
WE WATCH YOU AT YOUR HEARTH, WE WATCH YOU IN YOUR BED...

Tonight, Alfred, the shadows haunting Wayne Manor have come for me.
My goal--my only goal--is to reach you, my dear Son. And hold you again. But...
...should we never meet again in this lifetime, remember these simple truths.
Remember my love for you. Forgive me for all my many fatherly sins and know I tried my hardest to create a better life for you.
And remember, please, to fear Gotham City. Never visit, even in the event of my passing. This is a cursed place, a place that tricks you into loving it, into hoping... and the Wayne grounds, they are the most unholy of all. These lovely grounds...
...but I must hurry. I trust that if I should die, this warning will reach you and keep you safe from harm.
For ALFRED
With deep love and regret,
Your father
Jarvis Pennyw...

PRESENT DAY...
JARVIS PENNYWOR
JARVIS PENNYWORTH
THE FLOWERS ARE BEAUTIFUL, ALFRED. I'M SURE YOUR FATHER WOULD HAVE LOVED THEM.
I'M NOT SURE HE WOULD. HE NEVER DID HAVE TIME FOR MY LITTLE ECCENTRICITIES...ACTING, BOTANY...HE WAS ALWAYS PESTERING ME TO TAKE UP A TRADE MORE SENSIBLE FOR MY UPCOMING LIFE HERE AT THE MANOR.
AS IF ANYTHING COULD HAVE PREPARED ME FOR MY LIFE THESE PAST YEARS...CERTAINLY NOT MY FATHER, NO MATTER WHAT SHAPE HIS DEATH ACTUALLY TOOK.
SO THIS IS ABOUT MY FINDING THE PENNYWORTH NAME IN THE OWLS' LABYRINTH.
WE CAN LEARN THE TRUTH, ALFRED. UNEARTH THE BODY AND DETERMINE THE REAL CAUSE OF DEATH...
THIS ISN'T ABOUT CAUSE OF DEATH, MASTER BRUCE.
I WON'T DENY THERE'S A SPECTER OF DESIGN TO THE DISCOVERIES OF THESE LAST FEW WEEKS. THE REEMERGENCE OF MY FATHER'S NAME...

...A MAN WHO DIED VIOLENTLY A FEW WEEKS AFTER YOUR MOTHER MISCARRIED THE BROTHER YOU NEVER KNEW YOU LOST.
WHICH IS WHY I THINK IT'S OUR RESPONSIBILITY TO ACT.
WE ARE ACTING. EACH IN OUR OWN WAY.
I REMEMBER THE CLOUD OF DARKNESS WHEN I FIRST CAME TO THIS PLACE...AT THE TIME, I TRULY FELT THAT THE MANOR WAS CURSED. SOMEHOW HAUNTED.
I SUPPOSE IT WAS, IN A WAY. I IMAGINE THE ACCIDENT WOULD HAVE LOOMED LARGE DURING YOUR FIRST YEAR.
IT WAS MORE THAN THAT...DID YOU KNOW I NEVER CAME TO VISIT MY FATHER HERE? I BARELY KNEW HIM WHEN HE DIED.
AND YET, IN THOSE EARLY YEARS, I FELT HIM HOVERING OVER ME. LIKE A FORCE TRYING TO IMPART SOMETHING. BUT THERE WAS NOTHING I COULD DO BUT TRY TO LIVE UP TO THE MAN HE WANTED ME TO BE.
MY POINT, MASTER BRUCE, IS THAT I'VE ALREADY SPENT A LIFETIME TRYING TO DIG UP A SENSE OF WHO MY FATHER WAS.
I HAVE NO DESIRE TO LITERALIZE THE PROCESS.
IF THE COURT OF OWLS HAD ANYTHING TO DO WITH MY FATHER'S DEATH, YOUR ACTIONS THESE PAST FEW WEEKS HAVE BEEN TRIBUTE ENOUGH.

WE COULD KNOW FOR SURE, ALFRED...
BUT THAT'S JUST IT, MASTER BRUCE. I ALREADY KNOW EVERYTHING I NEED TO KNOW ABOUT MY FATHER.
JUST AS YOU DO ABOUT YOUR DECEASED BROTHER AND THE OUTLANDISH CLAIMS OF LINCOLN MARCH.
YOU KNOW I'LL FIND LINCOLN, ALFRED. I WILL FIND THE TRUTH.
YOU'LL FIND THE FACTS.
THE TRUTH IS THAT EVEN IF YOU AND LINCOLN SHARE THE SAME BLOOD, YOU STILL LOST YOUR BROTHER IN A CAR ACCIDENT WHEN YOU WERE JUST A BOY.
I KNOW YOU'LL DO WHAT YOU MUST, WHEN THE TIME ARISES.
BUT FOR NOW THE SPECTERS OF THESE LONG LOST KIN DESERVE TO REST...
...UNDISTURBED.
THE END

BATMAN #1 variant cover
by Ethan Van Sciver & Tomeu Morey

BATMAN #2 variant cover
by Jim Lee, Scott Williams & Alex Sinclair

BATMAN #3 variant cover
by Ivan Reis, Joe Prado & Rod Reis

BATMAN #4 variant cover
by Mike Choi

BATMAN #5 variant cover
by Chris Burnham & Nathan Fairbairn

BATMAN #6 variant cover
by Gary Frank & FCO Plascencia

# MORE BATMAN FROM DC

**BATMAN: YEAR ONE**
Writer: FRANK MILLER
Artist: DAVID MAZZUCCHELLI
ISBN: 9781401207526
$14.99 USA

**BATMAN: THE LONG HALLOWEEN**
Writer: JEPH LOEB
Artist: TIM SALE
ISBN: 9781401232597
$29.99 USA

**BATMAN: EGO AND OTHER TAILS**
Writer: DARWYN COOKE
Artists: DARWYN COOKE, PAUL GRIST, BILL WRAY, and TIM SALE
ISBN: 9781401213596
$17.99 USA

# MORE SCOTT SNYDER FROM DC

**BATMAN: THE BLACK MIRROR**
Writer: SCOTT SNYDER
Artists: JOCK and FRANCESCO FRANCAVILLA
ISBN: 9781401232078
$16.99 USA

**DARK NIGHTS: METAL**
Writer: SCOTT SNYDER
Artist: GREG CAPULLO
ISBN: 9781401288587
$19.99 USA

**BATMAN: LAST KNIGHT ON EARTH**
Writer: SCOTT SNYDER
Artist: GREG CAPULLO
ISBN: 9781779513182
$24.99 USA

# KEEP READING DC COMPACT COMICS

**BATMAN: HUSH**
Writer: JEPH LOEB
Artist: JIM LEE
ISBN: 9781779527264
Available now
$9.99 USA

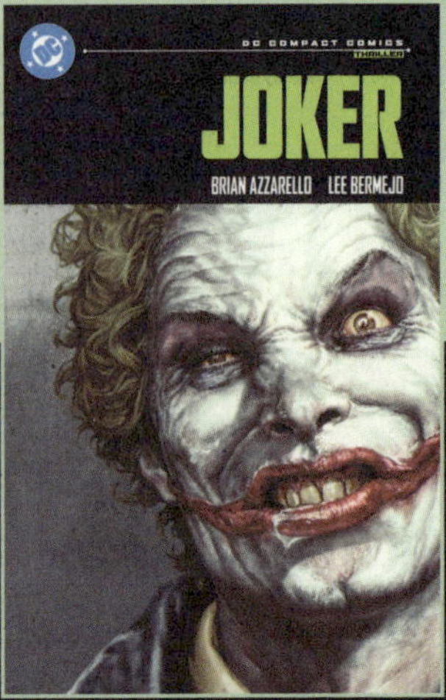


**JOKER**
Writer: BRIAN AZZARELLO
Artist: LEE BERMEJO
ISBN: 9781779527318
Available now
$9.99 USA

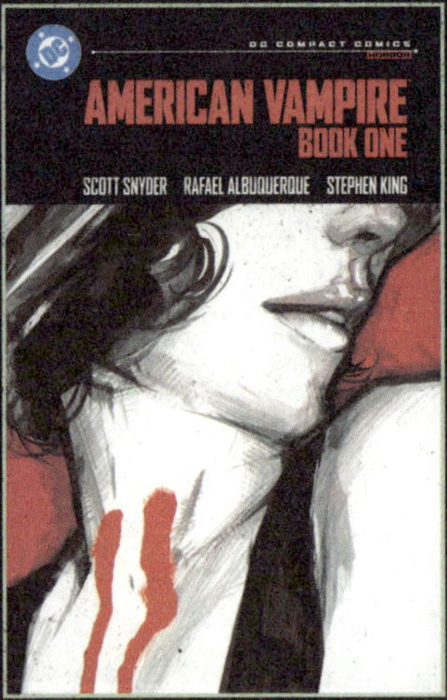


**AMERICAN VAMPIRE BOOK ONE**
Writers: SCOTT SNYDER and STEPHEN KING
Artist: RAFAEL ALBUQUERQUE
ISBN: 9781779527349
Available now
$9.99 USA

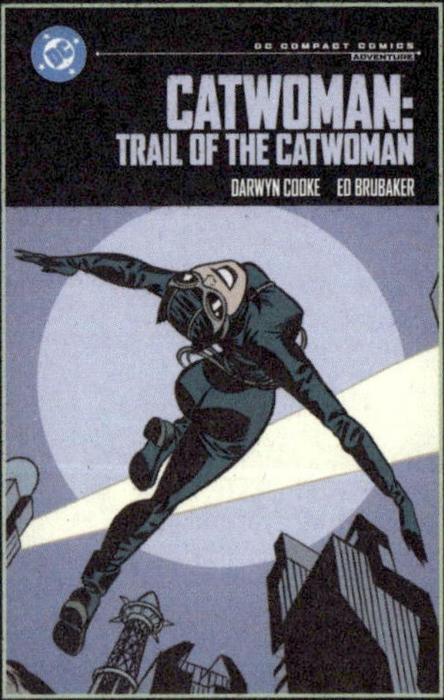


**CATWOMAN:**
**TRAIL OF THE CATWOMAN**
Writer: ED BRUBAKER
Artist: DARWYN COOKE
ISBN: 9781779527288
Available now
$9.99 USA